I had the great fortune to take guitar lessons from Jim for several years. Jims' gift for explaining musical concepts and techniques in straight forward, easy to understand steps makes him an ideal teacher... Highly recommended!

Marc Maddux

Jim Beckwith's Guitar system simplified a complex and often seemingly impossible…instrument.

Lawrence Duplantis III

Jim's system for switching chords and strumming is simple and easy to understand.

L. Kruse

Jim…has developed a unique system for teaching guitar…no matter what type or style of music one wants to learn.

Jay Lemoine

What people said about my book for beginners, No Fail Guitar;

The organization and flow takes the student through the basics while providing them with a system of learning that works.

Christopher Horrell

No Fail Guitar is a unique and sensible approach to learning the guitar, ... the process in this book is well thought out and gets the student efficiently to the business of making music. I use this as a resource for teaching guitar in a high school setting and find it very helpful.

Peter Whipple

TAKE CONTROL: For Guitar

Using Music Theory to Connect Chords, Scales, Songs, & Riffs Together to Achieve Your Goals

BECKWITH GUITAR SYSTEMS

Published by: Beckwith Guitar Systems

TAKE CONTROL: For Guitar
Using Music Theory to Connect Chords, Scales, Songs, & Riffs Together to Achieve Your Goals

BECKWITH GUITAR SYSTEMS

Published by: Beckwith Guitar Systems
PO Box 426
2300 Williams Blvd.
Kenner, La 70062-9998

www.beguitarsys.com

copyright © James Beckwith 2014

All rights reseved. Except for use in a review, no portion of this book may be reproduced in any form without written permission from the publisher.

ISBN# 978-0-9830298-2-3

Cover Design: Katherine Klimitas
Book Design: Katherine Klimitas and James Beckwith

Neither the author or publisher are responsible for any errors or omissions. Inclusion in this book does not constitute an endorsement by the author or publisher unless stated otherwise.

WARNING! This book was not written by an English major. Grammatical and punctuation errors are present. Proceed with caution.

Acknowledgements:
To my students, for *still* making me think! The Klimitas family for their hospitality and expertise. Rick Naiser at Festival Recording Studios. Family and friends. Thanks!

In Memory of My Mother, Winelle U. Beckwith

In Memory of My Mother, Winelle U. Beckwith

TABLE OF CONTENTS

PREFACE
Introduction — 7
The Foundation (Moveable Chords) — 11

THEORY
Introduction — 17
Chapter One: **Scale Construction** — 21
Chapter Two: **Chord Construction** — 27
Chapter Three: **Modes** — 33
Chapter Four: **Blues Harmony** — 39
Chapter Five: **Application** — 45

CHORDS
Introduction — 55
Chapter One: **Chord Theory** — 57
Chapter Two: **Chord Forms** — 67

SCALES
Chapter One: **The Basics** — 77
Chapter Two: **Using the Scale** — 83
Chapter Three: **More Scales** — 89

SUMMARY — 101
APPENDIX — 109

TRACK LIST

download audio tracks at www.beguitarsys.com

Track 1: Major/Ionian Mode	34
Track 2: Dorian Mode	34
Track 3: Triplet Pattern Position 1	84
Track 4: Riff #1	85
Track 5: Riff #2	85
Track 6: Riff #3	85
Track 7: Riff #4	85
Track 8: Riff #5	85
Track 9: Riff #6	85
Track 10: Generic Blues	86
Track 11: Generic Rock	86
Track 12: Performance Abbr. H	110
Track 13: Performance Abbr. P	110
Track 14: Performance Abbr. H/P	110
Track 15: Performance Abbr. B	110
Track 16: Performance Abbr. R	110
Track 17: Performance Abbr. B/R	110
Track 18: Performance Abbr. S	110
Track 19: Performance Abbr. ~ (Vibrato)	110

PREFACE

INTRODUCTION

> Quotation is a serviceable substitute for wit.
> -Oscar Wilde

Confused?

In the brave new world of the internet one thing is certain, you're not going to run short of information! Not so long ago, you had to pay for knowledge; scale & chord books cost money, so did song transcriptions if you could find them. Before that in the 60's, (I go back a long way), even books were scarce for guitar and song transcriptions were non-existent, basically you were on your own. Things are different now! Between the web, videos, and apps. you can find thousands of scales, chords and song lessons for free. While we can all agree that freely available knowledge is a good thing (it beats ignorance), I have a question. Have you learned it all? I bet I know the answer,

YOU CAN'T LEARN IT ALL!

3000 CHORDS! 1000 SCALE POSITIONS! 500 BLUES RIFFS EVERY GUITAR PLAYER SHOULD KNOW! Great, that's 4500 items, if you learned one a day that would take around *twelve years*! See you later! This is assuming you can retain them all or apply any of it. If this seems impossible, you're half right. You can't learn it all, what you need is a way to handle it. You need a system that lets you make intelligent choices about what to learn, understand how and why it works and relate it to what you already know. Also, to be useful and practical this system needs to be; simple, universal (works for all types of music), and most important, you must be able to apply it! You want a system that works for figuring out or composing songs, jamming and soloing etc., otherwise what good is it? You need a system that puts you in control.

MY SYSTEM

Over 25 years of playing and teaching, I have developed that system. I didn't set out to, it happened as I taught thousands of students of all ages and musical interests how to play and understand the guitar. I had to distill a university education and years of gigs into a simple, workable, and almost universal system, (It didn't work for Vietnamese temple songs). Let me define what I mean by simple, workable and universal.

- **Simple:** You can name all of the scales, chords and keys off of the two bar chord roots you probably already know! The total amount you need to memorize can range from two to six pages. People have built careers on less.

- **Workable:** Through out this book I will use excerpts from actual hit songs to illustrate my point and all chapters offer specific ways to apply this knowledge to your goals; figuring out songs, originals and soloing.

- **Universal:** By universal I mean popular music. This system covers about 90-95% of most popular music; rock, blues, country, pop, even a lot of jazz standards, and there are simple ways to handle the other 5-10%. If you are seriously into jazz or classical music, this system is a good foundation, but those styles need more than a few pages, so they are beyond the scope of this book.

HOW THIS BOOK IS ORGANIZED

This book has three main sections; theory, chords, and scales. All of these sections are short and to the point. I am focusing on what you need to function as a musician, memorization is kept to a minimum.

- **Theory:** tells how chords, scales and modes are built and function together as keys. I also explain modal interchange, another term for blues-based harmony. This is crucial to understanding rock and jazz, as well as blues. Not only will you understand how all of this works, but the 4 formulas I will give you can easily fit on one side of a 3 by 5 inch file card! This is so simple, I teach it to thirteen year-olds!

- **Chords:** Forget trying to learn thousands of chords, that will never happen! Instead, I will show you how to do what the professionals do; read and understand what the name is telling you to do, and modify some basic forms to get what you need. Six basic forms can produce almost a thousand chords! Like everything I teach, you can locate all of these from the two bar chord forms you probably already know.

- **Scales:** You can find thousands of scales and positions on line, which ones do you really need and how do you use them? The answer depends on how much you like to jam! If your goal is to solo all over the neck in several styles, maybe 12 to 15 positions. If you just want to get by, 3 or 4 positions will do the trick. Again, all of these scale positions can be located with the same two bar chord roots we use to locate everything else.

In addition I will have a short **SUMMARY**, that will show you how to tie all this information together and use it to reach your goals; whether figuring songs, jamming, developing lead styles or originals. Finally the **APPENDIX**, which will contain the basic diagrams and tables you can use for a quick reference, basically the 2-6 pages I said you needed to memorize!

WARNING! This book is not for complete beginners, I wrote a book called *No Fail Guitar* to deal with that challenge. I assume you can strum a few songs, know your two main types of bar chords (more or less), and maybe play a scale or two. Don't get me wrong, you can still learn a lot from this book, even if you can't play! You just won't be able to apply it on guitar. Also in spite of my sometimes breezy style, this book contains a lot of densely packed information! Go slowly and pay attention, many ideas will make more sense the second time around.

Introduction Summary:

- There is too much information available for you to absorb.

- You need a simple, easy to learn, practical system to deal with this information overload.

- I developed a system to do that over 25 years of teaching a wide variety of students. I know it works because they paid me! *This system bought my house!*

- This book is not for complete beginners.

If you've been feeling overwhelmed with too much stuff to learn and not enough time to do it all, give my system a try. It's short, simple, and most important, proven with thousands of students!

THE FOUNDATION

I must create a system or be enslaved by another mans'.
-William Blake

HOW THIS SYSTEM BEGAN

To put it kindly, this system took a while. When I first started learning guitar I was overwhelmed by the endless amount of stuff! After trying to memorize the entire chord encyclopedia (no luck there), I finally settled on learning a dozen more type I and II chords. I already knew the basics pretty well, so I figured I could learn a few of those 7ths, 9ths, and 6ths I kept running into. At least it was better than nothing. While I was at it, I got down a couple of scale positions to go with the two types of chords (I got these from friends, we didn't even know they were called pentatonic scales). Then, armed with this pathetic arsenal, off I went into the wide world of music! Lucky for me, standards were low back then. I drifted through several bands, first playing parties and dances and finally clubs by my senior year in high school. After stints at both the University of New Orleans and Berklee College, I finally began to get the picture. I settled back in New Orleans and began playing gigs, and after a year, I could support myself. I quit my day job unloading trucks and never did an honest days' work again! During all of this time, my total focus was on playing. All of my musical training was in theory and performance, I had no training in music education and no desire to teach. But a local music store needed a guitar teacher a couple of afternoons a week and it paid well, $15 an hour,(that was a lot in 1980), so I took a shot. I had 6 students ranging from an eight-year-old girl to a doctor in his 50's, with a few teenage boys thrown in. Before I taught my first lesson, I realized I had to make a decision. Would I teach the way I'd been taught? All of my lessons had been formal, involving music notation and jazz or classical examples. I was on my own as far as how to actually apply any of it to popular music, (it took a few years). I could have just taught songs, my ear was good and I knew some guys taught that way. Finally, I decided on a compromise, I would teach songs, but I would go further and show how the song worked, using scales and theory. This was the genesis of my system.

It was harder than I thought. I remember the dazed expressions as I tried to teach everything I knew about theory, or all 5 scale positions in one lesson. Those poor people. Still, I must have done something right, word spread and within a couple of years, I was teaching 40 students. Along the way, through trial and error, I developed systems to teach; beginner, scales and solos, music theory, chords, song transcription, even jamming. I refined those systems over two decades of full time teaching, (up to 90 students a week at one point). These systems had to work for a wide spectrum of ages and interests, because if they didn't, I wouldn't get paid! Over the years it slowly dawned on me that everything I taught was still based on the type I and II chords I had learned when I was 13! Somehow I had taken everything I'd learned over twenty plus years and made it fit the same basic concept I'd learned in 8th grade. It got even stupider, I began to relate everything, even theory and keys like a big picture. I realized it was much easier to teach everything visually. After all, it's how most people learn the guitar, they look at a picture of a C chord and play it, they don't worry about the theory behind it. It not only made it easier to teach keys, etc., it explained how completely self taught musicians could stay in key. Everybody was playing visually, apparently I was the last to know. To make it clear, I'm not just talking about chord or scale diagrams, I'm talking theory; keys, modes, altered chords, etc. Learning visually cuts your memorization to just a few pages and you don't have to "understand" anything! Just do it, as a famous philosopher once said. However, I will also teach you how things work, it will give you more flexibility if you know "why" and "how", as well as "what".

But first you must know the two main types of moveable bar chords and their root notes. Ultimately you will be able to locate everything from these notes. The faster you can find a chord, the faster you can find a scale or a key. So please look over the bar chord chart at the end of this chapter, it's all in alphabetical order and all the notes start to repeat at the twelfth fret. My system is simple, and it depends on these two types of chords and their roots, so the better you know them, the easier my system will be! Knowing type I/II roots is the *foundation* of my system.

Chapter One Summary:

- I'm a slow learner.

- My system is visual.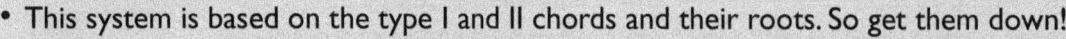

- This system is based on the type I and II chords and their roots. So get them down!

Speaking of getting down, lets get down to business! The next chapter starts theory...

Moveable Chords

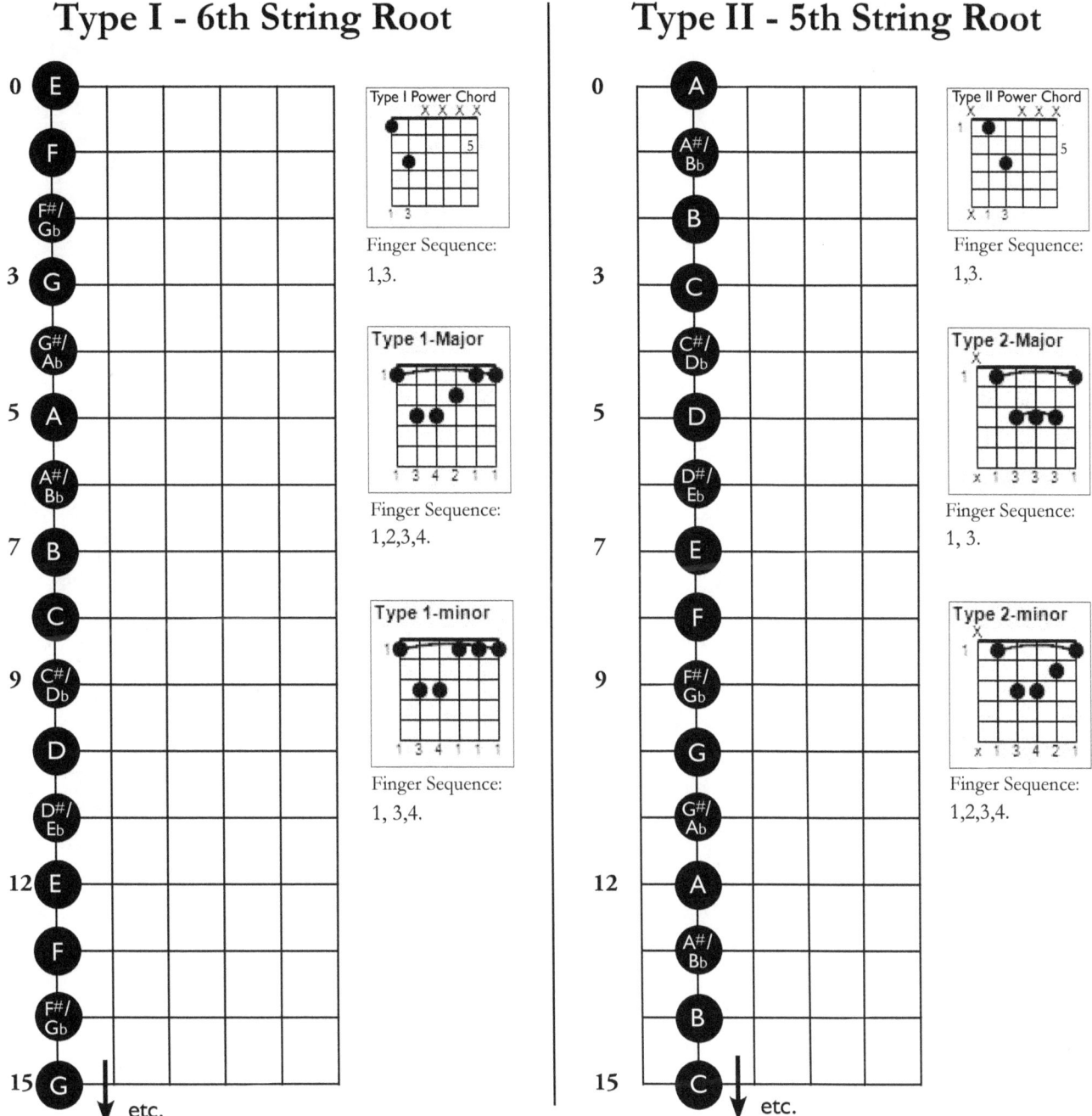

SHARPS AND FLATS

Those symbols you see on the chart above are called **sharps and flats**. Don't be afraid, they're just modifiers.

- **# Sharps:** Tell you to raise the chord one fret higher. *(For example, from the third fret to the fourth fret.)*
- **b Flats:** Tell you to lower the chord one fret. *(For example, from the fifth fret to the fourth fret.)*

The reason you see two names on fret four (in the Type I diagram above) is because it takes its name from the notes on either side. G# and Ab are the same note! You can call these notes either name right now, either G# or Ab. *(It will make a difference if you take a music theory class, but right now, who cares?)*

There are no sharp and flat notes between the B and C notes and the E and F notes. *(See Theory Lesson One.)*

PREFACE: THE FOUNDATION

THEORY

INTRODUCTION

Ninety percent of this game is half mental.
-Yogi Berra

OVERVIEW

So what is this "theory" anyway?

My definition of music theory is the study of how chords and scales are built and how they work together. This knowledge is what lets you connect all those separate bits of information; songs, riffs, chords, scales, etc., and filter out what's useless (to you). Practical application will allow you to actually use the good stuff you decide to keep. You can regain control over what you learn and build your knowledge base, not just a bunch of disconnected useless facts. Here is the most important fact about music theory, you don't have to use it!

Think of music theory as a set of tools, not a bunch of rules to follow. If you get a great idea for a song or a riff, don't worry if it's "correct"! Just play it and be happy for the inspiration. BUT, if you get stuck (what chords go with that riff?) you can use your theory tools to analyze what you just did and come up with options. If you're completely happy with everything you play, this book will make a good fly swatter.

KEYS: THE MAIN CONCEPT

My loose definition of a key is a group of chords and a scale that work together. The two types of keys we will cover in this book are major keys and blues keys. (Minor keys and major keys are just different ways to play the same key, a concept explained in the third lesson on modes). To illustrate my definition let's look at examples of both types of keys, starting on the note A. Here is the key of A major.

A Major

SCALE	CHORDS	MODES
A	A major	A Ionian (major)
B	B minor	B Dorian
C#	C# minor	C# Phrygian
D	D major	D Lydian
E	E major	E Mixolydian
F#	F# minor	F# Aeolian (minor)
G#	G# diminished	G# Locrian

- The left column lists the scale notes. Scales are used to play melody; lead guitar, vocalists, horn players and keyboards all use the same scales. This means you can learn horn riffs or vocal lines and play them on guitar, or vice versa, we're all using the same scale!

- The middle column lists the chords. Chords are used to play harmony; rhythm guitar and keyboards are the main instruments for harmony. All of the seven chords listed above sound good together and can be played in any sequence. True, some combinations sound better than others, but anything will work as long as we're in the key of A major. You don't have to play all of the chords either, just two or three are enough.

- Modes are the scary looking Greek words in the third column. Despite their mysterious names, they are just different ways to play the same scale notes and chords shown in the first two columns. Scales and chords are the only things you actually play in my system. The combination of chords and notes you choose to play will determine the mode you are in. Think of modes as a sound or a concept, not objects. You can play all seven modes with one scale position! *(Note that the Ionian mode can also be called major, and the Aeolian mode can also be called minor. Why this is, or what it all means, or what's with those flaky Greek names will have to wait for the lesson on modes.)*

So, the key of A major contains the 21 elements listed in the example above; a 7 note scale, 7 chords, and the 7 modes. You don't have to play everything, you can do just fine with two or three chords or scale notes. Anything and everything works! Now for the bad news, there are eleven more keys! One key for each note in the chromatic scale(which has twelve notes), and each key is different! Different scale notes, chords, and modes for each key! That's a lot to remember, and we haven't talked about blues keys yet.

The Key Of A Blues

SCALE	CHORDS	MODES
A	A major/A minor	generally, there are no modes in a blues key
B		
C	C major	
C# / Db		
D	D major/D minor	
D# / Eb		
E	E major/E minor	
F	F major	
F# / Gb		
G	G major	
G# / Ab		

Isn't *that* the craziest thing you've seen? This is not a miss-print, and I haven't just lost my mind,(I burned that out in the 70's). It is possible to play almost any note in a blues scale, and there are nine chords, some of which can be played as both major and minor chords. This may seem weird and impossible, but if you don't understand blues-based keys, half of all the music you learn will not make sense. I'm talking rock, modern country, pop, etc., not just blues or R&B. This is the fourth and in many ways the most important theory lesson.

You are probably feeling overwhelmed by now; twelve different major keys and twelve additional blues keys is a huge amount to learn, let alone memorize. The good news is you don't have to! You can learn the keys the way you learned a C chord, from a picture.

GETTING THE PICTURE

Memorization is for suckers, do you think BB King memorized this? How about *your* music heroes? My guess would be probably not, yet somehow they all sound great! Although it will disappoint you to learn I have not talked personally with every famous guitarist on the planet, I believe most of them work visually, off of shapes. Chord and scale shapes, which you probably know, and key shapes which you probably don't. For maximum understanding and flexibility we will learn our keys both ways, using theory, which tells how and why things work and visually, which shows you what to play. THEORY is split into 4 short chapters, *(a few pages each)* and a summary. The first three chapters deal with major keys and the final chapter is for blues-based harmony. Each chapter builds to the next, you must learn them in this sequence. Blues will not make sense if you don't understand modes, for instance.

- **Chapter 1-Scale Construction:** Tells how and why scales are built. Instead of making you memorize 12 scales, we use the step formula to make them. So instead of 12 things, you only have to learn one! Easy.

- **Chapter 2-Chord Construction:** Again, tells how and why chords are built. Making scales and chords is as easy as counting on your fingers.

- **Chapter 3-Modes:** The hardest thing about modes is spelling them. This simple idea can open up a whole new world of sounds, using the same chords and scales you already know! While many people understand scales and chords pretty well, most only partially " get" modes *(much less how to use them)*.

- **Chapter 4-Blues Harmony:** The most challenging concept to grasp, and still not taught in a lot of traditional schools. Blues harmony is simple if you understand the first three lessons. *(I didn't say playing the blues was simple!)*

- Summary: This shows you how to apply your knowledge. There are separate sections on using music theory to help figure out songs, write songs, learn riffs and solos, etc. Although these sections are brief and general they contain a lot of hard won and, I hope, useful hints that show how I use this knowledge every day. You can do all of these things without any knowledge of theory, it's just harder. I've tried both ways and I know.

Together, the information in these four chapters can be summarized on one side of a file card! This will be the total amount of memorization (for theory) I would like you to learn. However even that small effort is not really needed, since you can learn and play your keys by position, visually. The final part of the summary will show you how to do this. Although the truly lazy could skip all of the theory stuff and jump to this keys by picture part, actually knowing how things work can give you a lot more flexibility and control. So learn the theory!

Introduction Summary:

- Music theory allows you to connect the dots, build your knowledge base, and take control over what you learn.
- You **can** learn theory by position, but actually knowing how things work gives you a lot more flexibility.

CHAPTER ONE
Scale Construction

A handful of patience is worth more than a bushel of brains.
- Dutch proverb

WHY ARE WE DOING THIS?

There are two reasons to learn the names of the scale notes we are playing. One is to communicate with other musicians that aren't guitar players, (good luck telling the sax player to play the first string, third fret). But who really cares about them anyway? The second and most important reason is that the chords in the key are built off these notes! If we don't know the scale notes, we can't figure out the chords to play. So I guess we'd better learn the scale notes.

Key Signature: A Major

The standard method of learning the notes in a major scale is by memorizing key signatures, or lists of whatever # or b notes a particular scale might contain *(see example)*. The A major scale contains F#, C#, and G#, so that is its' key signature. This is a great way to learn your scales/keys if you're learning to read music notation, but we will not be. So, instead of requiring my students to memorize their keys, we use what I call the step formula to figure out the notes. This has two advantages; it reinforces the visual/physical aspect of scales, and it's easier to remember!

Are you ready? Here is your assignment, you must memorize this!

This is the *Step Formula*:
2 1/2, 3 1/2

Got it? Two and a half, three and a half. Repeat this several times until you can say with confidence, "two and a half, three and a half." Good! You have now memorized 25% of your theory. *(Not too hard so far, I hope.)* As many of you already know, the step formula is simply the distance between each of the notes in a major scale. I didn't invent it, I just use it to teach scales. For those who don't know what I'm talking about, here it goes:

The two in the formula refers to two **whole steps**, the half in the formula refers to a **half step**, etc. So the complete and more coherent way to pronounce the step formula is;

"Two whole steps, half step, three whole steps, half step."

This still doesn't make any sense unless you understand what the terms *"whole step"* and *"half step"* mean. They are just terms for the distance between two notes, on the guitar we measure that distance in frets.

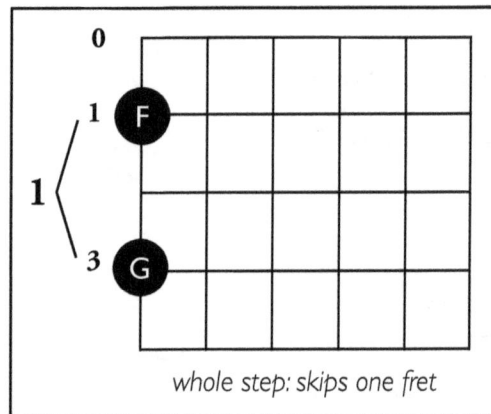

whole step: skips one fret

Whole Step: also called a whole tone, means skipping a fret on the guitar; an F on the 6th string, first fret and a G on the 6th string third fret are a whole step apart.*

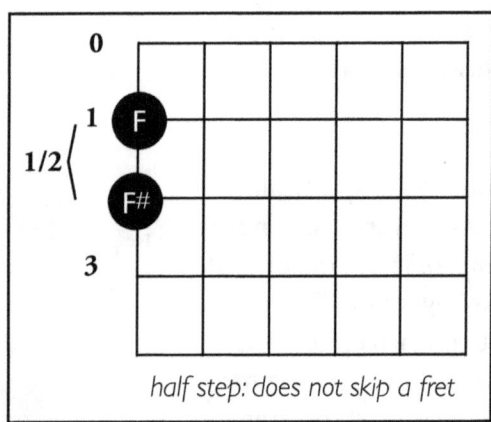

half step: does not skip a fret

Half Step: also called a semi-tone, means not skipping a fret on the guitar; an F on the 6th string, first fret and an F# on the 6th string second fret are a half step apart.*

*You can go in either direction, F to G is a whole step higher, G to F is a whole step lower. The same applies to half steps.

22   THEORY: CHAPTER ONE: SCALE CONSTRUCTION

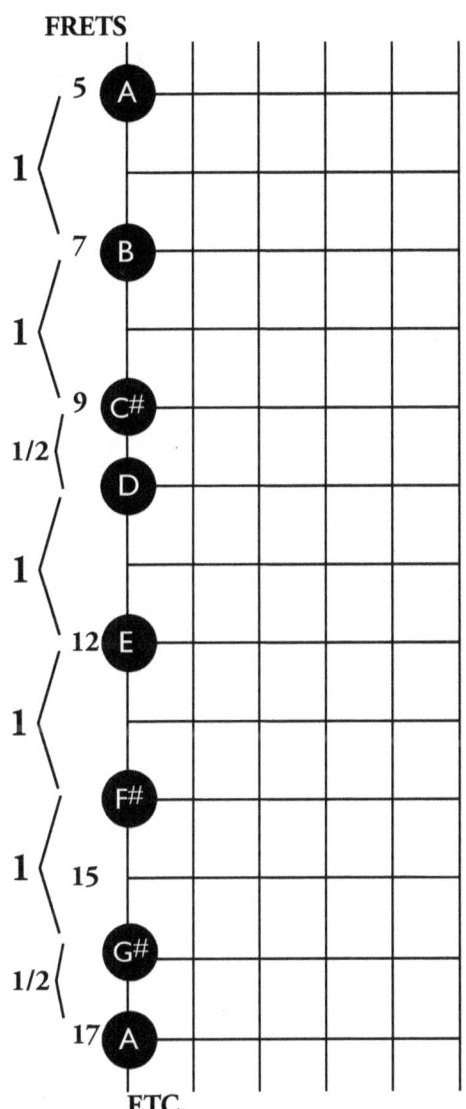

The illustration to the left shows the notes of an A major scale, laid out on the 6th string for easier visualization. Notice the one fret gaps between A & B and B & C# (two whole steps), while C# & D have no gap between them (half step). The rest of the scale completes the formula with three whole steps between D, E, F# and G# and a half step bringing us back to our root, A. Obviously, it's not too practical to play a scale like this, I'm just making it easier to see. *(You normally play scales in a position, across all six strings in a 4 or 5 fret area, it's easier to play and harder to visualize the step formula.)*

You can figure out the note names for any scale, using this step formula. In order to avoid careless mistakes, I use a 3 step process.

THREE STEPS TO WRITE ANY SCALE:

1. Pick the root note of the scale you want to play and write the letters of the musical alphabet below it *(the musical alphabet is just the first seven letters of our alphabet, A through G)*.

2. Put the individual numbers of the step formula in between the letters.

3. Modify the letters/notes to fit the formula.

THEORY: CHAPTER ONE: SCALE CONSTRUCTION

Let's try this with a different key, like Bb.

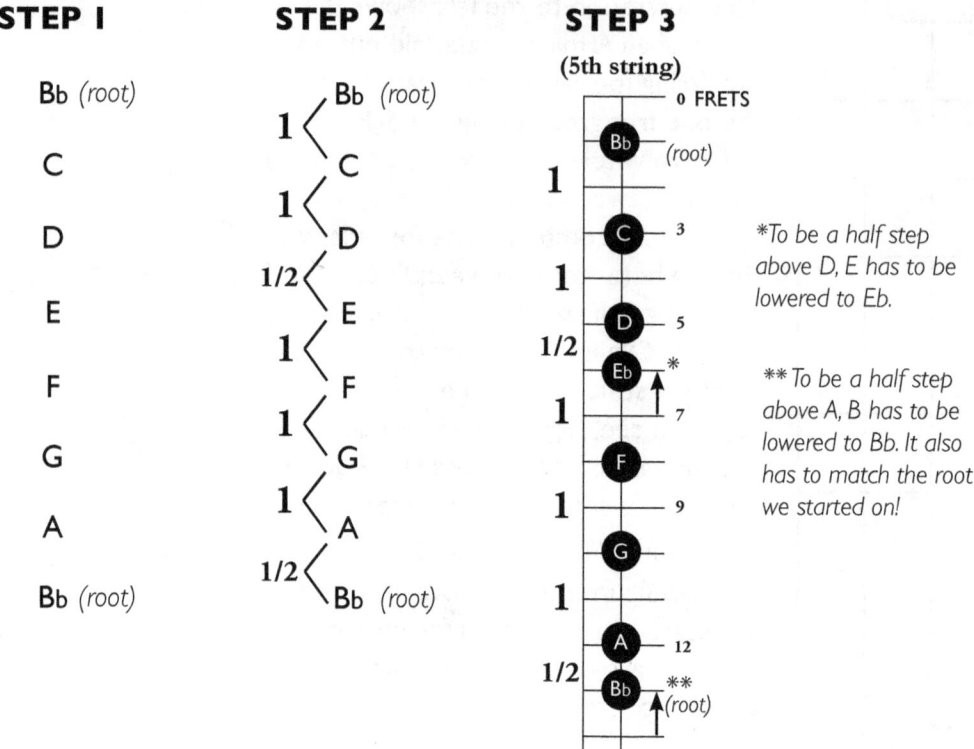

Step 1; write Bb, then skipping lines, write the rest of the seven letters. When you get to G, start over with A until all seven letters are used up and you're back to Bb.

Step 2; In the lines between the letters, fill in the whole and half steps from the step formula.

(two and a half, three and a half!)

Step 3; Until you complete this step you don't have a scale, just a bunch of letters and numbers. You have to make the letters/notes match the step formula. The easiest way to do this is along a string, like the example above. You can use any string, but in my system we only have to know two, the 5th and 6th. This time let's use the 5th string.

- Bb is on the 1st fret, and a whole step up we find C. OK so far.
- C is on the 3rd fret and a whole step up we find D. Easy cheesy.
- D is on the 5th fret and a half step up we find...uh... D#/Eb. Which name do we use? We use whatever letter we are on, in this case, E. So we call it Eb. (If we were on a D letter, we'd call it D#).
- Eb is on the 6th fret and a whole step up we find F. Back to natural notes.
- F is on the 8th fret and a whole step up we're on G.
- G is on the 10th fret and a whole step up brings us to A.
- A is on the 12th fret and the half step lands us back on Bb, fret 13. Notice fret 13 is the same as fret 1, everything starts over after 12 frets, so the last note has to match the first note.*

*Since we have written all seven notes in the scale, we start the entire process over on the number eight note, this is called an octave which means to play something twice as high or twice as low in the scale sequence.

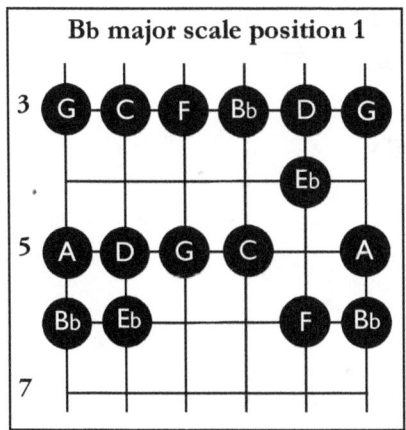

That's it! We've figured out the notes in a Bb scale. The only notes we alter are Bb and Eb, the rest are plain (natural) notes. As long as we're in Bb we play these same notes all over the neck, just in different octaves. Here is the Bb scale in position 1.

At this point, I ask my students to work out all twelve keys on a piece of scratch paper. You may want to try a few yourself, I have all twelve keys listed in the back so you don't have to, but as they say, "You're only cheating yourself". (I heard this a lot when I was younger, generally after I'd been caught cheating.) I have two final points:

1. NEVER, I mean *never* mix sharps and flats when you write a scale. Notice how A major contained only sharps, (F#, C#, G#)? Notice how Bb contained only flats, (Bb, Eb)? No major scale contains both sharps and flats. If that happens, you screwed up, start over.

2. In the appendix, you will notice that I have chosen keys starting on flat roots over keys starting on sharp roots. In other words, A# and Bb are the same note and therefore the scale built off that note would be the same, so why Bb? The answer is keys built off of sharp notes are almost always a lot more trouble to write correctly. If you look at the final diagram, you will see the Bb scale re-named as an A# scale. It's the same scale, which would you rather pronounce?

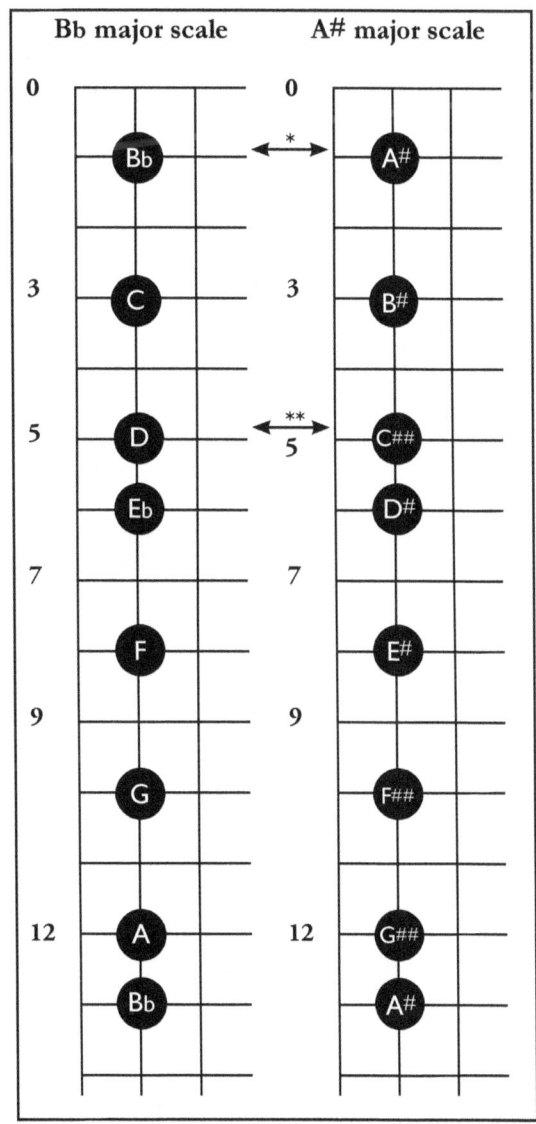

*All notes must be on the same frets with different letter names.

**Yes, you can sharp a note TWICE!

* In the appendix you will also notice I did include two sharp rooted keys; F#, (the same as Gb) and C#, (the same as Db). The reason for this will not be clear until the lesson on blues harmony, trust me for now.

THEORY: CHAPTER ONE: SCALE CONSTRUCTION

Chapter One Summary:

- If you can remember "two and a half, three and a half", and you know your type I and type II chord roots, you can find the notes to any major scale!
- Once you know the scale notes, you can find the chords.

This is probably a good time to talk about chords, in the next chapter...

CHAPTER TWO
Chord Construction

> We're drowning in information and starving for knowledge.
> -Rutherford D. Rogers

A *chord* is defined as at least three different notes played together. You can strum them all at once and create *harmony*, or play the notes separately (melodically, like a scale). The two main instruments for playing chords harmonically are guitars and keyboards. Everyone else has to play the notes separately, in an *arpeggio*. An arpeggio means playing the chord notes one at a time instead of strumming them together. You can't strum a C chord on a trumpet, so you play the C arpeggio instead.

In this lesson, you will have one concept to learn and seven words to memorize. Let's start with the main concept:

CHORDS ARE BUILT IN THIRDS OFF THE SCALE

You probably don't know what that means. That's OK, we'll figure it out in a few minutes, just say it for now, "chords are built in thirds off the scale". Easy enough. In case you haven't figured it out yet, the seven words to memorize are the seven chords in any major key;

MAJOR, MINOR, MINOR, MAJOR, MAJOR, MINOR, DIMINISHED

This chord sequence is the same for any key. You take the seven note scale you figured out in the scale lesson and match the note names to the chord names listed on the previous page, always in the same sequence, and Ta Da! You've just named the seven chords for that key. The example below shows this process using the two scales we made in lesson one:

MATCH SCALE NOTES TO CHORD NAMES

Key of A Major		Key of Bb Major	
SCALE	CHORDS	SCALE	CHORDS
A →	A major	Bb →	Bb major
B →	B minor	C →	C minor
C# →	C# minor	D →	D minor
D →	D major	Eb →	Eb major
E →	E major	F →	F major
F# →	F# minor	G →	G minor
G# →	G# diminished	A →	A diminished

Notice that even though two scales are different, the chord sequence is the same. Also notice that we are through with the practical part of this lesson! If you can remember the seven chord sequence above, you can match it to any major scale you know and come up with the chords for that key. (You can play them too, if you have the type I/ II page down.) All twelve keys are listed in the appendix, but I ask my students to start writing their own keys by copying the scales from the scale lesson and adding the chord names from this lesson. The repetition helps reinforce the step formula and chord sequence. The rest of this lesson is devoted to understanding how chords are made and named, and *why* they all work together in a key. To do this, we go back to the main concept listed in the beginning of this chapter:

CHORDS ARE BUILT IN THIRDS OFF THE SCALE

The word "thirds" in the above sentence refers to an *interval*. An interval just refers to the distance between two notes. In this case a third interval means you skip one note in a scale.* In the A scale on the next page, the scale notes A and C# are a third interval apart, you skip the B note. It doesn't matter what scale or what notes in the scale, or which direction, if you skip a note you have a "third". Now that we have defined what "thirds" means, we can start making chords! (I assume you know what the other seven words in the concept mean.) Let's build the first two chords in the key of A;

*If you skip two notes in a scale, it's called a fourth, etc. There are interval names for every conceivable distance between two notes. A complete study of intervals is a hassle and doesn't help us, so I'm ignoring it. The only interval I care about is a third, which means skip a note in the scale.

Building Chords In Thirds

SCALE	CHORD NAME: ARPEGGIO	SCALE	CHORD NAME: ARPEGGIO
A	A major: A ^{2} C# $^{1\,1/2}$ E	A	
B		B	B minor: B $^{1\,1/2}$ D ^{2} F#
C#		C#	
D		D	
E		E	
F#		F#	
G#		G#	
(A)		(A)	

Getting the notes of the A major chord in the example on the left was easy. I just started on my root note A, skipped the B note to C#, and skipped the D note to E, (ie., I built in thirds). These three notes; A, C# and E, make up an A major chord. (Strummed together they are a chord; played separately, an arpeggio.) Since an A major chord contains only three different notes, it's also called a triad. You can play these three notes in any sequence and even double up (or triple!) notes, as long as you have at least one of each note. Notice the two chords from the type I/II chart with the notes spelled out underneath:

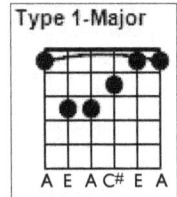

Type I A Major:
5th Fret

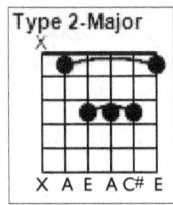

Type II A Major:
12th Fret

The B minor chord in the right example at the top of the page follows the same procedure. I started on my new root note B, skipped the C# note to D, and skipped the E note to F#. These three notes; B, D and F#, make up any B minor chord; strummed, separate, any combination or sequence, etc. Again, notice the type I/II examples.

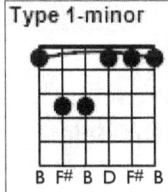

Type I B Minor:
7th Fret

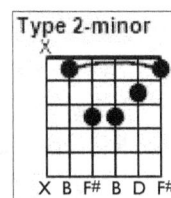

Type II B Minor:
2nd Fret

THEORY: CHAPTER TWO: CHORD CONSTRUCTION

...And so on and so forth. Just keep doing this building in thirds process on each of the five remaining notes in the A major scale, and you have built all seven chords. The next example shows all seven chords spelled out in the key of A major. Notice the last three chords; E major, F# minor, and G# diminished require you to go into the next octave higher to spell them easily.

Building Chords in Thirds

SCALE	CHORD NAME: ARPEGGIO
A	A major: A ^{2} C# $^{1\ 1/2}$ E
B	B minor: B $^{1\ 1/2}$ D ^{2} F#
C#	C# minor: C# $^{1\ 1/2}$ E ^{2} G#
D	D major: D ^{2} F# $^{1\ 1/2}$ A
E	E major: E ^{2} G# $^{1\ 1/2}$ B
F#	F# minor: F# $^{1\ 1/2}$ A ^{2} C#
G#	G# diminished: G# $^{1\ 1/2}$ B $^{1\ 1/2}$ D
(A)	*(A major: A ^{2} C# $^{1\ 1/2}$ E)
(B)	(B minor: B $^{1\ 1/2}$ D ^{2} F#)
(C#)	↓
(D)	*Etc. After the seventh diminshed chord, the cycle starts over again.

(Scale intervals shown between adjacent notes: 1, 1, 1/2, 1, 1, 1, 1/2, 1, 1, 1/2)

This is why the scale and chords work together! They're the same thing! Either you play the scale notes separately or strum them together in a chord, it's all off the same group of notes.

There's one last question to answer: If we're building all of the chords the same way, (in thirds), why are some chords called major and others minor or diminished? I'm glad you asked! Chords have their own step formulas. If you look at the A major arpeggio in the example above, you will notice a 2 in between the A and C# notes. That's because A and C# are two whole steps apart in the scale. (Check the step formula next the notes, there are two 1's between the A and C# notes.) The 1 1/2 between the C# and E means a step and a half between the two notes. *Any* chord with this 2 whole step, 1 1/2 step sequence is called a major chord! Check the D major and E major arpeggios, same thing. *Minor* chord arpeggios reverse this sequence, 1 1/2 steps between the first and middle notes, 2 whole steps between the middle and last notes. The dinky diminished arpeggio has 1 1/2 steps between all three notes, making it the smallest chord to spell out and the weirdest sounding. This chord naming step formula is also the reason the chords are always in the same order; major, minor, minor, major, major, minor, diminished. Since all major scales follow the same two and a half three and a half step pattern and all chords are built in thirds off of this pattern, you will always get the same result, no matter what key! Same scale pattern, same building in thirds process, same chord sequence.

Chapter Two Summary:

- Don't worry if the previous paragraphs make your head hurt. You can either keep reading them over and compare all those step formulas until it makes sense, (it will eventually), or you can ignore it all and just be happy knowing there is a reason! The chords and scale notes of a key are related, they have to work together.

- The only thing you have to remember is:

MAJOR, MINOR, MINOR, MAJOR, MAJOR, MINOR, DIMINISHED

CHAPTER THREE
Modes

Whatever is good to know is difficult to learn.
-Greek proverb

Key of A Major

SCALE	CHORDS	MODES
A	A major	A Ionian/Major
B	B minor	B Dorian
C#	C# minor	C# Phrygian
D	D major	D Lydian
E	E major	E Mixolydian
F#	F# minor	F# Aeolian/Minor
G#	G# diminished	G# Locrian

Modes confuse a lot of people, mostly because of the Greek names. However, the basic concept is simple:

A mode tells you which chord or note of the key you're in is the root* of the song.

*Root- By root I generally mean the first and last chord or note in the progression. Also played the most in the progression, it all comes back to the root.

In the key of A, if the root chord is an A major, you are in A Ionian mode. Your song can go to any other chords in the key;

you are in A Ionian mode. If you change the root chord to B minor:

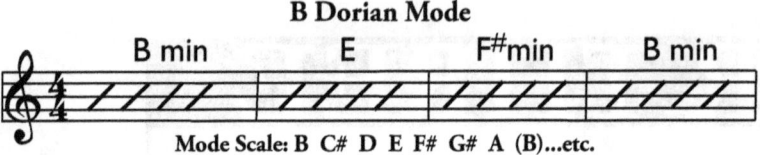

you are in B Dorian mode. Same thing if you play a scale; play an A major scale from A to A, you're playing A Ionian mode. Play the same A major scale from B to B and you're playing B Dorian. The mode names match the number names, the first chord is always an Ionian root, the third chord is always a Phrygian root, etc. *(check the keys in the appendix).* Pros use the term *degree* to describe a note or a chords' place in a key, so you will often see Ionian mode referred to as starting from the first degree of the key, or Phrygian starting from the third degree of the key. Remember, degree equals the number in the scale sequence. Easy!

At this point, most students have two things pop into their minds:

1. That seems easy.
2. BFD, or "what's the point? If it's the same scale and group of chords and all I'm changing is the root, why do I care and why do I have to give it a hard to spell Greek name?"

Position 1: A Major/Ionian Scale
(first 3 strings only)

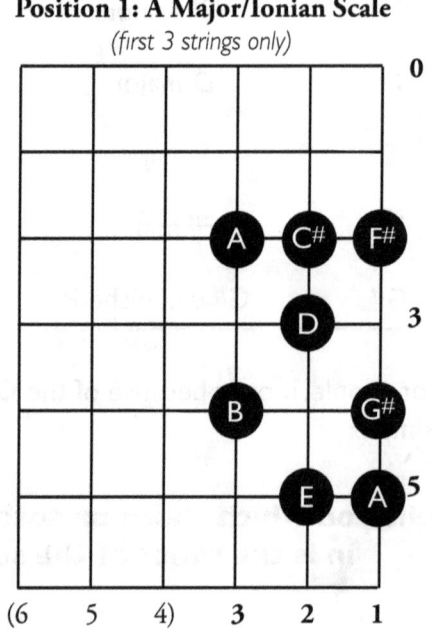

I'm glad you asked! By basing the chord progression or scale around different degrees, you get entirely different sounds. Dorian modes sound different than Phrygian modes, even in the same key. You can get seven different sounds (one for each mode), from the same key! To illustrate this, try playing a simple A major/Ionian scale over the following two chord progressions:

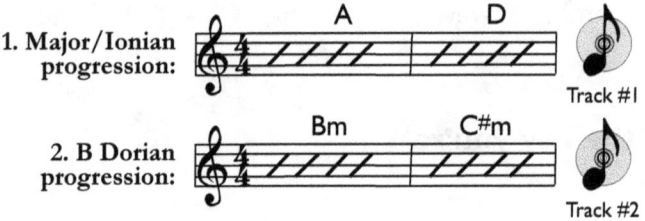

34   **THEORY:** CHAPTER THREE: MODES

Don't do anything fancy, just play the same dumb scale back and forth over the two different progressions like I'm doing in the examples. In example one, you get the nice, bland major sound we all know and love. In example two, the sound shifts to a jazzy minor using the same scale! *This* is why modes are important. Understanding modes allows you to get seven different sounds, some quite exotic, using the same scale! In fact, if you're playing over modal chord changes (with the correct root), like examples one and two above, *all* you need to do is play the scale. The chords will give you the modal sound. If you are playing the scale by itself, you will have to start and stop on the correct root. After all, *somebody* has to play the correct root. The easy way to do this is to count up the number of notes from the root of whatever scale you are playing. In the example, if I wanted a B dorian sound I would just start and stop on the second note of the A scale. The more I emphasize the B root, the "more dorian" I sound. Try playing the scale from B to B (dorian), then A to A (ionian). Many books treat modes like separate scales, but it's all the same scale, just different roots. If you want to be a Mode Master, and you have lots of time to practice, go ahead and practice playing the major scale from all seven roots. I'd rather not. If somebody asks me to jam in E mixolydian, I just play an A major scale and locate my riffs around the E note, five notes up from the A major root. Works for me!

Position 1 with Mode Roots
(any key)
(first 3 strings only)

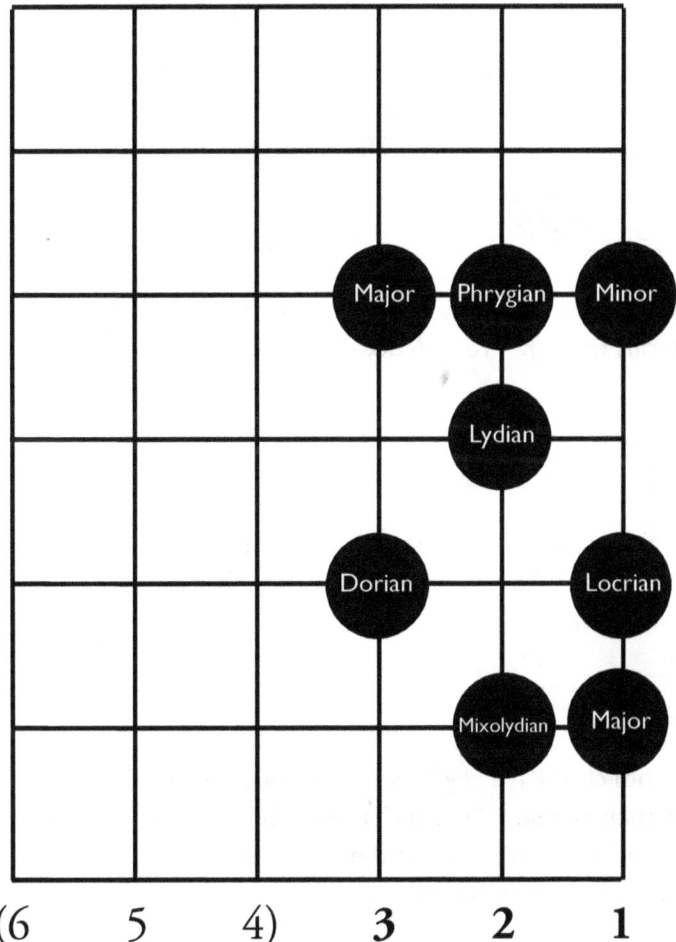

THEORY: CHAPTER THREE: MODES

Here is a brief and highly subjective summary of the seven modes, their tonal qualities and a simple two chord progression to jam over. *(We've already covered the first two.)* You can play the same scale on page 34 for all seven examples and emphasize the different mode roots listed on page 35. Seven sounds from one scale!

Ionian mode: Also called Major mode, always based on the first chord in a key. Ionian has the "happy", bright sound we think of when somebody says "major". Used in a lot of country, pop and jazz standards. Examples are "When I Come Around" (Green Day), "Jambalya" (Hank Williams), etc.

| A | D |

Dorian mode: Always based on the second chord in a key. Used in Celtic folk songs, also has that jazzy minor sound. Both "Eleanor Rigby" (Beatles) and "Evil Ways" (Santanna) have a dorian sound.

| Bm | C#m |

Phrygian mode: Always based on the third chord of a key. The flamenco scale, adds drama. Used not only in Spanish style tunes but heavy metal (the drama thing). Both "Malaguena", and the solo to "Wherever I May Roam" (Metallica), work in phrygian.

| C#m | D | | C# * | D |

*Sometimes the root is changed to major, to make it even stronger. Yes it's technically out of key, so what!

Lydian mode: Always based on the fourth chord in a key. Lydian is used by jazz players to solo over major keys because it sounds hip. It's also used in cartoons, because it sounds both happy (like a major mode), and tense (like things might get crazy!). The Simpsons cartoon theme has a Lydian sound.

| Dmaj7 | Amaj7 |

Mixolydian mode: Always based on the fifth chord in a key. Bluesy but exotic. Good for adding interest to rock solos. The main riffs to both "Pretty Noose" (Soundgarden) and "Tom Sawyer" (Rush) are in mixolydian.

| E | D |

Aeolian mode: Also called Minor mode, always based on the sixth chord in a key. Aeolian has the "sad" sound when we think "minor". It's also used in a lot of rock songs, like "Stairway to Heaven" (Led Zeppelin), or "Runaway" (Dion).

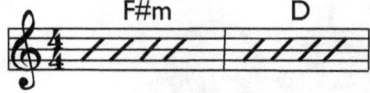

| F#m | D |

Locrian mode: Always based on the seventh chord in a key. This scale is tense, because the root chord is a diminished. Pretty impossible to use in "normal" music, I hear it used by fusion bands like Mahavishnu Orchestra, and death metal bands the kids bring in. Fun to play just to see how weird you can make a major scale sound!

| G#°7 | B°7 |

This lesson only scratches the surface of modes. I'm just explaining enough to show how they work, practical applications like soloing (can I play mixolydian over AC/DC?) or composing will have to wait (see Superimposing Modes in appendix). You only need to understand two things for this lesson. We've covered the first, ie., modes are just different ways to play the same key or scale. The second thing requires one more brief explanation:

WHY MODES HAVE GREEK NAMES

Because the Greeks discovered them. The Greeks discovered the concept of getting different sounds over the same scale by using different roots. They named the modes after tribes and regions in ancient Greece. Why those names? Who knows, they're dead! But they discovered them so they named them and we still use them. You will notice the first and sixth modes have two names. That's because those are the only two modes used in 99% of modern music, so we gave them modern easy to pronounce names. Ionian became Major mode and Aeolian became Minor mode. Apparently nobody else wanted to pronounce the Greek names either! (Except the Greeks). This brings us to the second concept:

MODES AND KEYS ARE THE SAME!

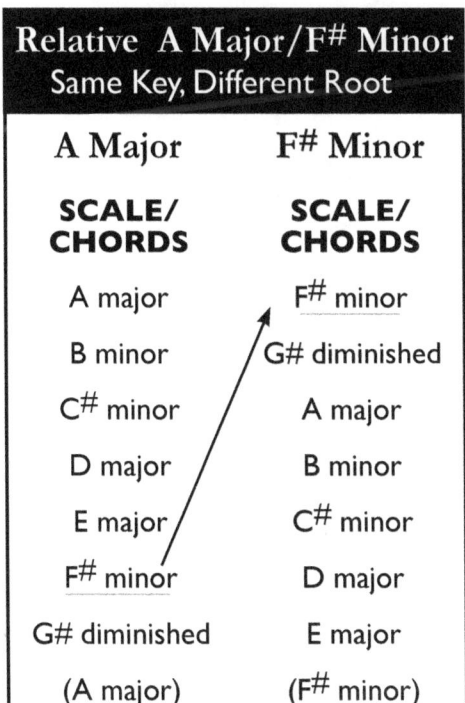

If you want to get picky, they aren't exactly the same. Mode generally refers to the modal scale by itself (just the notes). Key refers to both chords and scale together (the whole package). However, most people don't care, Dorian mode is used to refer to both the modal scale and the chord progression. This is important when you consider the first and sixth modes. The *modes* of Major/Ionian and Minor/Aeolian are also called the *keys* of Major/Ionian and Minor/Aeolian! Major keys and Minor keys are the same thing, just different roots. This means you not only know your major keys, you know your minor keys, just look on the sixth line of the key chart!

The only difference between the key of A major and F# minor, is in the key of F# minor, the first chord is F# minor (root), the second chord is G# diminished, etc. The scale and chords are all the same, only the sequence is different. These two keys, A major and F# minor, are sometimes called *relative* major and minor keys because they are the same group of notes and chords, played from different roots. So if you want to know where all the minor keys are in the appendix, look on the sixth line!

Parallel A Major/A Minor
Same Root, Different Key

A Major	A Minor
	(C Major)
SCALE/ CHORDS	**SCALE/ CHORDS**
A major	A minor
B minor	B diminished
C# minor	C major
D major	D minor
E major	E minor
F# minor	F major
G# diminished	G major
(A major)	(A minor)

The example to the left shows the keys of A major and A minor. Although they both start on the same note A, they are not the same key. A minor is related to C major, check the appendix if you need to. They may start on the same root note but but major and minor keys start on different degrees, so they have to be in different keys. These are called *parallel* keys, same root, different keys.

Chapter Three Summary:

Modes can seem complicated, but they aren't if you understand two things:
1. Modes just mean playing the same chords and scale over different root degrees.
2. The terms Modes and Keys are used interchangeably by most; Major mode=Major key. Minor mode=Minor key.

Since most popular music is written in either major or minor, memorizing the rest of the modes can wait. As long as you remember that major keys are based on the first degree and minor keys are based on the sixth degree, you're good!

CHAPTER FOUR
Blues Harmony

> There is a road from the eye to the heart that does
> not go through the intellect.
> -G.K. Chesterton

WHY BLUES IS IMPORTANT (even if you don't like Blues)

Because rock comes from blues, as well as R&B (guess what the B stands for) and jazz. Basically all modern popular music contains at least some blues element. If you don't understand blues harmony about *half* of all popular music will not make complete sense. The previous three lessons; scales, chords, and modes are all traditional music theory. This is what's taught in most introductory music classes, and it's fine for a lot of classical music, folk songs and some popular songs. But if you listen to rock, modern country rock, R&B, smooth jazz, etc., traditional music theory starts to fail. If you want to understand what's going on, and not just guess and hope for the best, understanding blues harmony is crucial. This is still not taught in a lot of traditional schools and it's one reason I went to Berklee. Here is all you need to know about blues harmony:

BLUES = MAJOR + MINOR MODE

Parallel E Major/E Minor	
E Major	**E Minor** *(G Major)*
SCALE/CHORDS	SCALE/CHORDS
E major	E minor
F# minor	F# diminished
G# minor	G major
A major	A minor
B major	B minor
C# minor	C major
D# diminished	D major
(E major)	(E minor)

A blues key mixes *parallel* major and minor keys together, it's major and minor at the same time! (It's a candy mint *and* a breath mint.) For example, a song based in E blues harmony can contain notes and chords from both E major mode (key of E), *and* E minor mode (key of G), mixed together! Yes, this means up to fourteen chords are possible, along with almost every note on the guitar! Before you burst into tears let me reassure you, it's not that bad. Mostly.

More than 90% of blues based songs only use the major chords from both keys (for a total of six chords). The less than 10% remaining songs also use a minor chord or two, and that's from a specific group of three chords, bringing the chord total to nine. *(See worksheet below.)* And while a blues scale can contain a lot of notes, most people just use a pentatonic minor scale and add a few extra "blues" notes as needed. The next part of this lesson will focus on using chords to identify blues harmony, while the last part will cover the blues scale.

Blues Key Worksheet
with most commonly used chords from both keys

E BLUES KEY

chords from key of E major	chords from key of E minor/(G major)
E, A, B	G, C, D, E min., A min., B min.

HOW DO I KNOW IF A SONG IS IN BLUES HARMONY?

It's far easier to analyze a songs' key by looking at the chords, instead of scale notes. I can tell a songs' key knowing only three or four chords. Once I know the key, I know the scale as well as the rest of the available chords. This makes figuring out the rest of the song easier. No matter what kind of popular music you listen to, there's a 50/50 chance some blues harmony will creep in. The more "rock" it is, the more likely blues harmony; the more "pop", the more likely it's in major.

> **If a song is in a major key;** things are easy, I can find the first three or four chords in one of the twelve major keys. For example, "Don't Stop Believing" by Journey starts with these four chords: E, B, C#m, A, etc.

The key is not clear until the fourth chord A major. The first three chords can be found in both the key of B or the key of E, but the A major chord means we're in the key of E. Now that I know the song is in the key of E, figuring out the rest of the song is easier. I have a short list of seven chords to pick from, (I probably won't use them all), and a scale to use for lead soloing. However,

> **If a song is in blues harmony;** I start running into problems, the chords stop working! By that I mean I start getting chords that aren't in the key, in fact they aren't in any major key! Let's look at the three main problem areas...

THREE "PROBLEMS" THAT BLUES HARMONY SOLVES

1. **"Too Many" Major Chords**: If a song has more than three major chords, it can't be in a major key ,(major keys only have three major chords, as well as three minor and one diminished). If a song has four or more major chords, I'm probably in blues harmony. Here are some examples in E blues harmony:

> Example 1: Both "Steppin' Stone" (Monkees) and "Take It Away" (The Used) contain: E, G, A, and C major chords.

> Example 2: "Rock You Like a Hurricane" (Scorpions) contains the same four chords and adds a D major.

You can't find the major chords for these songs in any single major key! Check all twelve keys in the appendix if you want. You can only find these chords in E blues, *(Check the E blues worksheet on the previous page.)* How did I know it was E blues? Because E major was my root, and there were too many major chords. Notice none of these songs sound "bluesy"! Remember, rock comes from blues.

2. **Major Chords in the "Wrong Spot"**: Wrong spot means I can't find the major chords in any regular major key, even if there are only two or three. For example, I knew the two previous songs were in blues harmony by the second chord. No major key has both an E major and a G major chord. An example in a different blues key is the boogie pattern used by John Lee Hooker, ZZ Top, Canned Heat, etc., which contains A, C, and D major.

At first glance you might think this was a major progression, because there are only three major chords. Good luck finding them in a major key! Only A blues harmony contains them.

Blues Key Worksheet
with most commonly used chords from both keys

A BLUES KEY

chords from key of A major	chords from key of A minor/(C major)
A, D, E	**C**, F, G, A min., D min., E min.

3. **Those Pesky Minor Chords**: So far I've been talking about major chords being the problem, and they are the main culprits 90% of the time. But the three minor chords listed in the blues key work sheets in the examples above can also cause double takes. For instance, sometimes the same chord can be major and minor! A lot of 50's music does this:

Although having both D major and D minor in the same key seems impossible, it works in blues!

Blues Key Worksheet
with most commonly used chords from both keys

D BLUES KEY

chords from key of D major	chords from key of D minor/ (F major)
D, G, A	F, Bb, C, **D min**., G min., A min.

WHERE'S THE ROOT?

These three "problem areas" let me know I'm in blues harmony. All I have to do then is locate the root chord to determine the blues key. Most of the time the root chord is the first main chord in the song. However in a small percentage, like two percent, it's the last chord. An example is "Hey Joe" (Billy Roberts/Hendrix), which contains C, G, D, A, and E major chords (when played in the key of E).

Hey Joe is not in C blues, it's in E blues! The chords can't even be found in C blues and the C blues scale doesn't work. This is rare, and the only time I see it is when the last chord is held the longest. (In "Hey Joe," the final E is held for eight beats.) This covers the main part of blues harmony, ie., chords, now it's time to discuss the scale.

THE BLUES SCALE

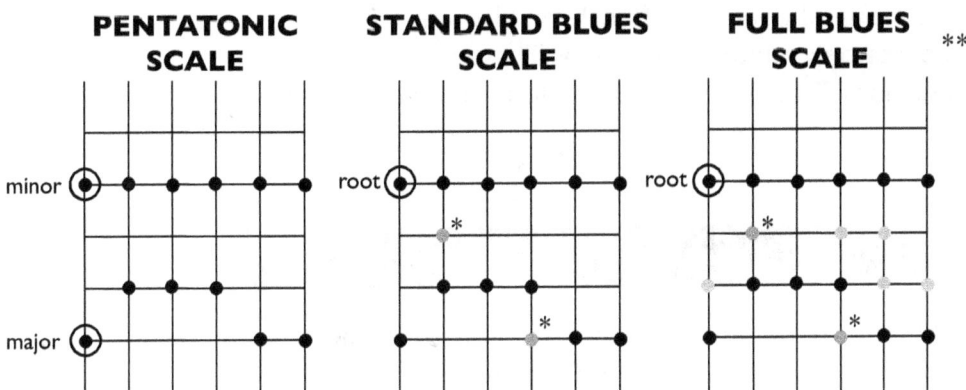

*b5 (the passing note between the 4th and the 5th intervals in the scale)
**Even more notes are possible, but outside of the position.

You have probably noticed that the blues scale I show has more notes than the standard blues scale seen in most books. This is because the standard blues scale is nothing more than a pentatonic minor scale with a b5 added. If you've played a few blues or rock solos, you know there's more to it. Adding the extra major and minor notes gives you a lot more options. Check out these two examples:

Blues Riff in the Style of the Allman Brothers
G Blues (scale fret 3)

Rock Riff in the Style of Alvin Lee, Jimmy Page, etc.
A Blues (scale fret 5)

THEORY: CHAPTER FOUR: BLUES HARMONY 43

Notice they didn't play every note available! Both riffs are mostly pentatonic minor with an extra blues note added. The blues "scale" I recommend is not so much a scale as a pentatonic minor scale with a group of options. In fact, if you play it as a full blues scale it sucks! So think of it as a pentatonic minor with options. These extra notes can be added to all five pentatonic positions, listed in the appendix. Just don't dump them all in at once!

Chapter Four Summary:

- The distinctive sound of blues is the sound of major and minor being played together. The blues worksheets illustrate this, and you can find them at the bottom of the key pages in the appendix.

- Blues harmony is the fourth and final theory lesson. In the summary chapter that follows we will learn how to use it and the rest of basic theory to deal with practical problems. I will also answer a couple of questions you might have, namely; How can I memorize all of this? and, Where's that file card you mentioned in the theory intro?

CHAPTER FIVE
Application

> Originality is nothing but judicious imitation.
>
> -Voltaire

USING THEORY TO TAKE CONTROL:

Knowledge without the ability to apply it is useless. This section will show examples of how I use my knowledge of theory to help with real musical challenges. Until you use it, all the previous information I've presented will not make a lot of sense. At the start of this book I promised help in several areas; figuring out songs, song writing, solos, and jamming. Let's get started!

1 - FIGURING OUT SONGS

Although you can find the music for a lot of songs not everything is available, even note detection software is not always reliable. Sometimes, if you want to play it, you have to figure it out! If you are truly starting from scratch, you will have to start by ear. I wish they started every song by telling me the key, but they never do! Learning to find chords by ear is a skill that takes work to develop, and is beyond the scope of this book to cover completely. For now we'll assume you can pick out a few chords by trial and error, (and if you can't, check out the appendix for some hints!).

I always start with the chords when I'm first figuring out a song. Chords are easier because there are only six or so possible chords in a key and the notes could be anywhere, so it's chords first. I also skip over any intro section or pickup notes and start with the first main part, ie. the verse or the chorus. Generally it takes between two and four chords to learn what key the song is in, three chords is average. If a song only has three chords, or two chords it's more ambiguous and I have a little detective work to do. All music transcription involves trial and error, the more experience the less trial and error. Here is my process to find the key:

- **Song has more than three chords:** Relatively easy, I should be able to find them in one of the twelve keys (major or blues). Here are some examples:
  - **Who'll Stop the Rain** *(Creedence Clearwater Revival)*: KEY OF G MAJOR
    (Chords: G, D, C, Em, etc.)
  - **Glycerine** *(Bush)*: KEY OF F MAJOR   *(Chords: F, C, Dm, Bb, etc.)*
  - **Dirty Deeds** *(AC/DC)*: KEY OF E BLUES   *(Chords: E, G, A, D, etc.)*

  After the third chord it's pretty obvious what key I'm in, although at first you may have to look at them all to decide.

- **The song only has 3 chords:** Sometimes the chords can be obvious like the boogie pattern in the blues chapter (A,C,&D chords, key of A blues), or a simple hymn like Amazing Grace (G, C, & D chords, key of G major). Sometimes the chords can be ambiguous, belonging to more than one key. I see this a lot with blues and 50s rock, since twelve bar blues contains the same I,IV,V major chords that a lot of folk/pop/country songs use. For example both Johnny B Goode (C. Berry) and He Stopped Loving Her Today (George Jones).

  If played in the same key both songs will use the same three chords(A, D, & E), but JB Goode is in A blues and He Stopped Loving Her Today is in A major! Since there are no other chords to figure out, the only reason I need to know the key is find out which scale to use when I solo. The short answer is I can use either scale over both songs, because if the chords and scale match they have to work together. (Read that again if you have to). It's not a question of what works, it's a question of what's appropriate. JB Goode is a rock song, so a blues scale is better. He Stopped Loving Her Today is a country song, so a major scale is better. When in doubt, play both scales and see!

- **The song only has 2 chords:** I also see this in some three chord songs that don't fit the blues/major stuff in example two. Now is when my knowledge of modes comes in handy. Although I know from experience that most two chord songs use the the I and V chords, that's not a guarantee, so I will look for the most "normal" mode to tell me what my key is! Examples are Jambalaya/Tulsa Time/ Achy Breaky Heart.

  These are typical two chord songs, for example Jambalaya played in the key of C contains a C major chord and a G major chord. Discounting blues keys, because of style, I can still find these chords in both the key of C and the key of G! The root chord is C major, so if I'm in the key of C that makes it a C major/Ionian mode(C is the first degree). If I'm in the key of G and C major is still my root, I'm in C Lydian (C is the fourth degree in G). I'm guessing Hank Sr. didn't jam in Lydian, so I'll go with C major! So if a song is in two different keys, look at the root chord and check out the mode: normal song means normal mode, weird song means weird mode. By the way, C lydian, (a G scale), will work over Jambalaya! If the chords and scale match it has to work, so go ahead and play C Lydian over Jambalaya, you pervert!

ONCE YOU KNOW THE KEY

Once you know the key it gets easier, but still not easy! You will still have to use trial and error, only now you have a short list of seven chords (if you're in a major key), or six to nine chords (if you're in a blues key). Every time a chord changes, it should only take five or six tries maximum to find the next one out of that short list. Again, the more you do the less trial and error. The key will also tell you the scale to use to figure out solos or jam in. I will cover this in following sections. While this covers the basics for finding the key/chords, occasionally you may find yourself screaming...

THEORY: CHAPTER FIVE: APPLICATION

THE #@! CHORDS STOPPED WORKING!

If that short list of chords stops working, it means the song changed key! Songs do that sometimes, especially long or complex ones. This means you have to start over and figure out the first two or three chords completely by ear again, to learn the new key. Or you can pick another song that's easier. I'm serious, figuring out songs is a challenge even with easy songs, so start simple. Find songs with a few chord changes and the guitar mixed up front, and save the hard songs for later.

2 - SONG WRITING

Nothing beats a flash of inspiration when you're writing a song. Out of nowhere, a cool riff pops into your mind and in a few minutes you're playing it. No amount of theory will ever substitute for creativity, but theory can help! If you know the key your cool riff or chord progression is in, then you have a list of other chords and notes available to help you write the rest of your song. You find the key by looking at the notes in your riff, or chords in your progression, and seeing what scale/key contains them. You might find them in more than one key, so try both keys and see which group of notes and chords you like better! Theory won't write your song for you, but it will give you options. Actually there are rules for composing "pleasing" melodies and chord progressions, but if you resort to them your song will sound like a toilet paper commercial. If you're lacking inspiration, a better strategy might be to...

STEAL YOUR SONG*

> There is a difference between imitating a good man and counterfeiting him.
> -Benjamin Franklin

OK, "steal" might be too strong a term, how about " inspired by" or "recycled"?

Lots of hit songs are "recycled" from previous hits. After all, if an idea was good enough to sell a million records twenty years ago that idea should still work! Your goal is to tweak the original enough so its not too obvious and avoid any legal action. Besides the obvious steps like changing the lyrics and melody, you can change the key, alter the tempo and feel, even change the instruments. Changing the key is easy, just use the degree names of the chords and make a direct switch to another key. Songs using the "circle pattern", (I,vi,IV,V) are a good example. (The Roman numbers are explained in *visual keys*, at the end of this chapter.)

- **Every Breath You Take** *(Police)*: KEY OF A   *(Chords: A, F#m, D, E)*
- **Earth Angel** *(Penguins)*: KEY OF C   *(Chords: C, Am, F, G)*
- **Baby** *(Justin Beiber)*: KEY OF Eb   *(Chords: Eb, Cm, Ab, Bb)*

All of these songs, along with thousands more, are based off the same type of chord pattern. Why? Because it sounds good! Notice none of them sound alike, that's the creative part. If all you do is change the key, you will get sued!

> *This is just my attempt at humor. I don't encourage you to steal anybody's material, nor am I implying that any of the artists mentioned in this book did anything improper.*

3 - SOLOS AND JAMMING

Once you know what key you're in, you have the scale to use. Remember this book is for popular music styles, not jazz, fusion, or classical. More challenging music has more possibilities and requires more knowledge than what's in this book. I will cover jamming in the appendix and developing your own solo style in the scale section. For now, let's look at figuring out the existing solos and riffs in the song you just learned the chords to.

LEARNING SOLOS AND FILLS

Transcribing lead solos is hard work, most musicians never get this skill down. It's easier to find the tabs, video, music, etc., or use note detection software and hope for the best. Still, not all solos are available and learning your own solos is a worthwhile skill to develop. It will make you more independent as a musician and improve your ability to hear notes and play them. This is GOOD. Since learning to pick out the notes in a solo is a long and winding road, the most useful thing I can do is give you some tips to shorten the journey.

- **Tip #1:** Start easy! This may seem obvious, but don't start with a five minute long, tour de force technical masterpiece that will take ten pages to write out. Pick short, easy to hear, not too fast solos to begin with. When these start getting easy, move up in difficulty.

- **Tip #2:** Cheat! Thanks to the wonders of digital technology, you can use a wonderful device called a phrase trainer that will allow you to slow down a solo to half speed! These are available for purchase (Tascam makes one), or even free apps, for smartphones, if you have one of those (Tempo Slow is one app.). These also allow you to loop a phrase over and over until you get it. Just look up "phrase trainer" and see what pops up.

- **Tip #3:** Don't assume the key! Sometimes solos are in a different key than the rest of the song, it makes them stand out. Always figure out the chords and the key for the solo section first. Be sure! (This will not be a problem for easy songs).

- **Tip #4:** When figuring out solos, try position one* first. I call this basic position, because it's the easiest to play and you have at least a 50% chance that the solo will be in this position. It's my default position, when I figure out a solo I try this position first. Also if the notes are awkward to play, try shifting to the next position up or down, the fingering should get easier.

- **Tip #5:** You can often find fills in the scale notes around the chord the fill is played over. For instance, if a fill is played over a D minor chord, just play the notes in that chord, along with any other scale notes around it.

- **Tip #6:** Take it in small bits. You really can't learn a twenty note phrase. Split it into several four or five note sections and learn those. You wouldn't be intimidated by a four note lead solo, would you? This is where the looping feature on the phrase trainer I mentioned in tip number two comes in handy. A fast, twenty note riff might seem impossible but a half speed four note chunk of it, not so much.

*see scale section.

SUMMARY

Knowing the theory behind musical keys; major, minor, and blues, helps you to understand music in new ways. Chords and scales go together for a reason, and already we have learned how to use theory to help figure out and understand existing songs and solos. When you learn a song and understand it, you know a lot more than just a song. You can take riffs, even entire chord progressions and put them into new keys and incorporate them into your musical vocabulary. While you may sound derivative at first, everybody does. As you rework these ideas through jamming and playing they will become a part of your unique style. The next section will deal with chord theory. While this may produce yawns right now, it will be worth it, I promise. Speaking of promises, at the beginning of this book I made two claims;

#1: All of the facts necessary to write the twelve keys could fit on one side of a file card.

#2: It's possible to locate all of your keys visually, you don't have to know theory!

THE FAMOUS FILE CARD

If you know your type I and II bar chord roots, and read and mostly understood the previous four chapters, that's easy!

Note this isn't an actual file card, just a picture. If it makes you feel better you're welcome to cut it out and glue it on an actual file card.

SCALE FORMULA	CHORDS	MODES
1	Major	**Major**/Ionian
1	Minor	Dorian
1/2	Minor	Phrygian
1	Major	Lydian
1	Major	Mixolydian
1	Minor	**Minor**/Aeolian
1/2	Diminished	Locrian

Blues Harmony = Parallel Major+Minor Mode

Just use the step formula to find the notes from either of your bar chord roots, plug in the chords and modes to match and remember to use parallel* major and minor modes to figure out blues harmony.

Parallel means same root, different key, if you don't understand this reread the chapter on modes!

THEORY: CHAPTER FIVE: APPLICATION

VISUAL KEYS

If all this theory gives you a headache and even the file card is too much hassle, you can find the chords in your keys by position. Since scales are built from a physical pattern (the scale step formula), and chords are built off the scale notes, it seems logical that the chords in a key will follow a similar pattern. As I said in the intro many players do this, including some greats. Below are the seven chords in the key of A major starting from a type I root.

VISUAL MAJOR

Notice I have written it two different ways; the left is actual chord names and the right uses scale degrees to name the chords. If you learn the pattern with scale/chord degrees, you can start it anywhere on the fret board and get any key you want! Notice I use Roman numbers to name the chords, see the section below to learn how to read them.

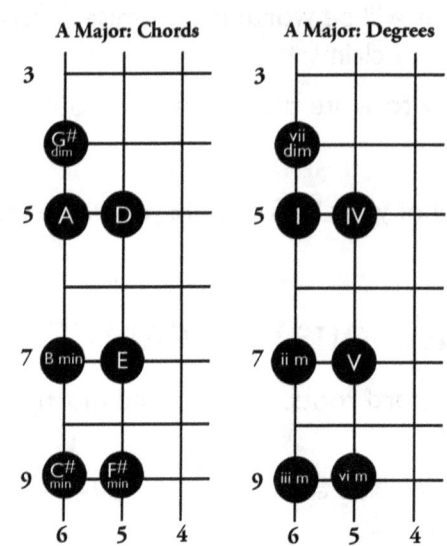

Chord Degree Names

Chord Degree Names Use Roman Numbers:

- Uppercase Roman numbers (I, IV, V) mean major chords.
- Lowercase Roman numbers (ii, iii, vi) mean minor chords
- Lowercase plus degrees sign (vii°) means a diminished chord.

For more, see "Chord Degree Names" in the appendix.

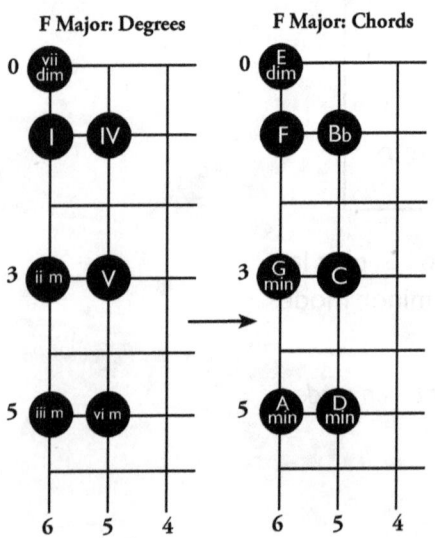

Need the chords for F major? Move the pattern to the F root/type I on the first fret and you get all seven chords for the key of F.

You aren't limited to just the seven chords in the pattern, obviously. If the pattern says you can play a C major chord you can play any C major chord you know, not just what's in the pattern.

VISUAL BLUES

The blues key looks a little different, as you might guess. Here are the nine chords in the key of A blues starting from a type I root. Again I have written the pattern as both actual chord names and scale/chord degrees, so it can be moved.

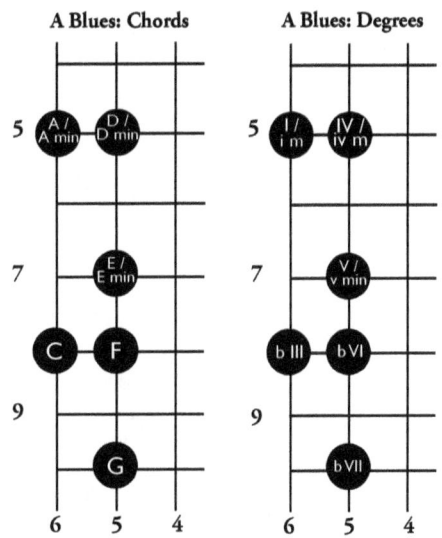

This time we'll just do the key of B blues.

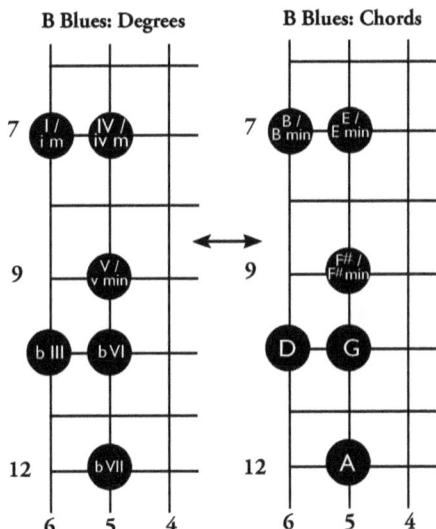

You don't have to locate the chords from the type I root, the type II root works as well, and I've shown the key shapes from both types of chords in the appendix. You also don't have to have the chords only listed above the root, as I did in the examples above. You can list the chords below the root as well, although the pattern will be different you will still get the same chords. (This is in the same chart in the appendix.)

While it's useful to know the key pattern from both types of chord roots all over the neck, and to be able to move the pattern to any key, you really only have to know the minimum patterns I showed you first. With just these two small pictures and your type I and II roots you can figure out the chords in any key! (And after you read the scale section, you'll be able to do the same with scales.)

THEORY: CHAPTER FIVE: APPLICATION 51

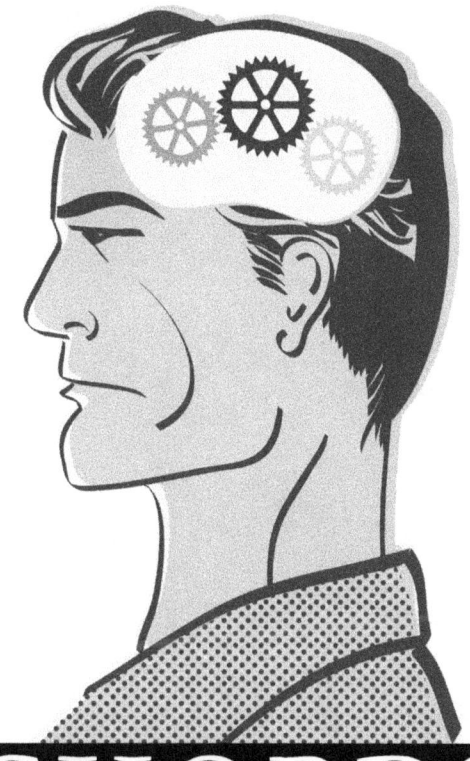

CHORDS

INTRODUCTION

I am a deeply superficial person.
-Andy Warhol

HOW YOU CAN BECOME CHORDMONSTER OF THE UNIVERSE!

Most guitarists find chords impossible to master. After all there are thousands of chords, many with complex names and some of them sound pretty weird. A decent sized chord dictionary can contain over five thousand chords! If you learned one new chord a day, it would take you almost 14 years to get them all down, (that's if you remember them). That's a lot of work just to be able to play an Ab7#5b9 chord in case somebody asks! Even if you could play it, how would you use it? It's no wonder most guitarists learn the basics and fumble with a chord book or app. for the rest. What most professionals know that amateurs don't is that the name of a chord is actually a *formula*, that tells you how to make the chord! The average guitarist has no idea what a chords' name stands for, that Ab7#5b9 might as well be called Suzy for all they care. For a pro however, any chord name is just a set of directions. They can read the chord name, pick a basic form, and modify that form whatever way the name tells them to. This makes your job a lot easier!

Instead of learning thousands of chord forms, you just have to learn how to understand the chord name, learn a reasonable number of basic Type I/II forms, (twelve besides the two basic forms in the front of this book), and you can make over 1000 chords! That should be enough, but even if some evil person slips in a chord that's not covered, you will be able to either work it out or fake it. While fourteen chord forms may still seem like about twelve forms too many, it's a small price to pay for this amount of control and flexibility. Get this down and you too will become, CHORDMONSTER OF THE UNIVERSE! Here is a visual representation of what you need to know in order to do this...

The first part of this lesson will teach basic chord theory. This part builds on the chord lesson presented in the theory section of this book, so if you didn't get that down, now would be a good time. The second part shows the fourteen basic forms, how to modify them and some examples for application.

CHAPTER ONE
Chord Theory

An expert is a man who has made all the mistakes,
which can be made, in a very narrow field.

-Niels Bohr

HOW TO READ A CHORD NAME

In order to read and understand a chord name, you have to know two basic premises and the names and formulas for nine chords. You don't even have to know this in order to play the thousand plus chords I promised at the start of this chapter! You can do all of that by position just as I laid out in the beginning of this book. However, if you understand what it is you are doing, you can substitute chords and figure out any weirdo chords I didn't cover. The more you know, the more flexibility you have.

The first premise was presented in the basic chord lesson...

Premise #1: Chords are built in thirds, off of the scale.

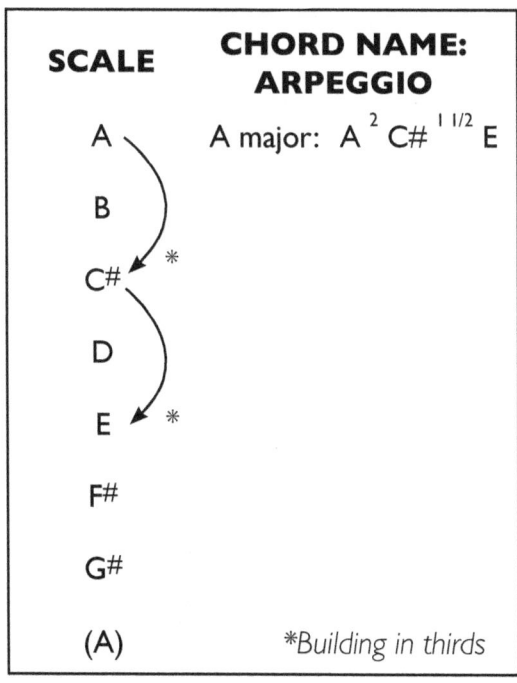

Remember this just means to skip every other note in the scale, like we did for the first example in that chapter, making an A major chord in the key of A.

What I didn't say in that lesson was that this building in thirds process can be continued until we use up *all* the notes in the scale! This is how to do it:

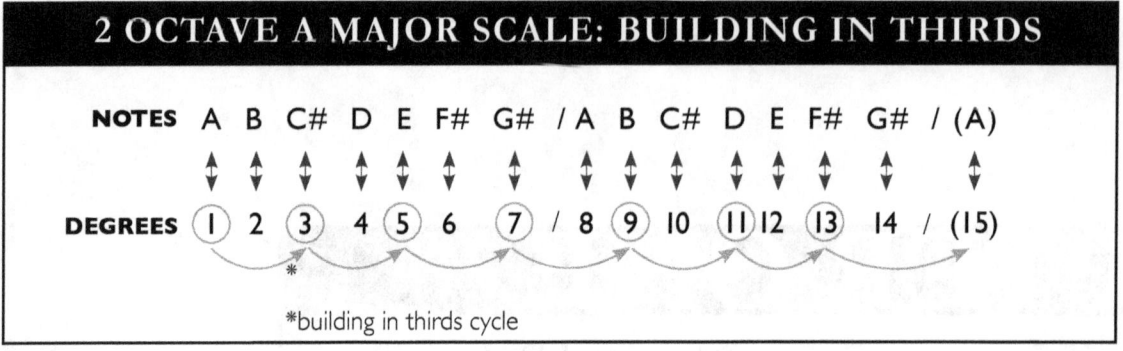

*building in thirds cycle

Notice I gave degree numbers to all of the scale notes in the first octave (1 through 7 like before), but when I got to the second octave *I didn't start over*, I continued the number/degree sequence 8 through 14 until the end of the second octave. You will also notice that if I keep building in thirds, I will eventually use up all the notes in the scale, the numbers I miss in the first octave I get in the second octave; #2 B becomes #9 B, #4 D becomes #11 D and #6 F sharp becomes #13 F sharp. This explains all those odd numbers in a chord name, they just tell you how far up the "building in thirds" cycle the chord is going! For example, the A major chord above is called a triad because it goes up the "building in thirds" cycle for three notes.

A major

1   3   5   =   A   C#   E

DEGREES = NOTES

But an A major 7 chord goes up the cycle for *four* notes!

A major 7

1   3   5   7   =   A   C#   E   G#

DEGREES = NOTES

Care to guess what an A major 9 is? an A major 11? an A major 13?

A major 9

1   3   5   7   9   =   A   C#   E   G#   B

DEGREES = NOTES

A major 11

1   3   5   7   9   11   =   A   C#   E   G#   B   D

DEGREES = NOTES

A major 13

1   3   5   7   9   11   13   =   A   C#   E   G#   B   D   F#

DEGREES = NOTES

This explains why you never see any chord numbers higher than 13, because 15 just starts over at A, and you already played that! For the same reason you'll never see an 8th chord,(or a 10th, 12th, or 14th chord since those numbers have already been used as 1,3,5 and 7). This premise still leaves a lot out, like what are 6th chords and sus4 chords, and how can I play a 13th chord with only four fingers? Hang on, that information is on its way later in the chapter. Before we do that, we need the second premise...

Premise #2: The scale used to build the chord is always named from the root of that chord.

When you're reading a chord name you don't care what key you may be in, you always use the same scale as the chord root. For naming purposes the chord is in its own little world. Consider the following little song, in the key of C and containing the following three chords...

We use three different scales to figure out the chords!
- Dminor7: Use a D scale to figure out chord notes
- G13: Use an G scale to figure out chord notes
- Cmajor7: Use a C scale to figure out chord notes

Notice that even though the song was in the key of C, the only time we used a C scale was for a C chord. Naming chords has nothing to do with keys, although it works off the same principles, you are in chord land now! This wraps up the two premises, so you may want to pause and get a refreshing beverage before the next section. This section will explain how to read and understand a chords' name, and show the formulas to make 4 triads and 5 seventh chords. (The 9 chords I mentioned at the beginning of this chapter.)

HOW TO READ A CHORDS' NAME

4 BASIC TRIADS

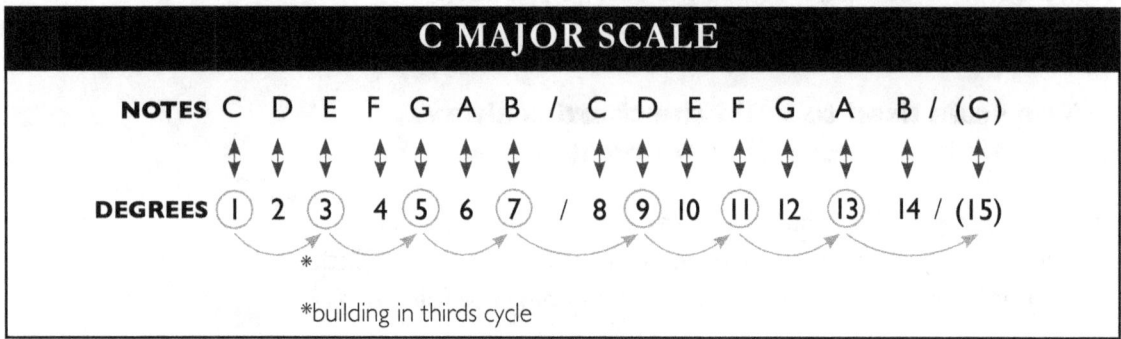

TRIADS		
NAME	DEGREE FORMULA	STANDARD ABBREVIATION/ PRO SYMBOL
C MAJOR	1 3 5	C / C
C MINOR	1 b3 5	C min. or C m. / C-
C DIMINISHED	1 b3 b5	C dim. / C°
C AUGMENTED	1 3 #5	C aug. / C+

About Power Chords:
Strictly speaking power chords are not chords at all, since they only contain two notes. Their "correct" name is a perfect 5th interval, which nobody pays attention to. They are abbreviated with a 5; E5, A5, etc., means they want a power chord.

The four chords listed above are the simplest, most basic chords you can play. *All* chords, no matter how complex, are based on these four chords. They are called triads because they only go up the chord building cycle of thirds for three notes, (as mentioned before). If you want to know what notes are in a chord, you have to know its degree formula. For C major, play the first, third and fifth notes of a C scale; C, E, and G. For a C diminished, flat the third and fifth notes; C, Eb, and Gb. You can play these three notes in any sequence, double up on notes, it doesn't matter. As long as you play at least one of each of those three notes, you have that chord. This is called *voicing* a chord, a chord voicing is just a specific arrangement of its notes. Equally as important as knowing a chords' note formula, is knowing how to read the name. After all, if you can't read it you can't play it. Chords are almost never written out in full, it would take too much space, instead they are abbreviated. To add to the confusion you may encounter two different ways that chords are abbreviated; standard (the way most people would shorten a name), and a mysterious symbol that pros use (because it's faster). For even more "fun" sometimes the two styles are mixed! Notice that in both standard and pro abbreviations, C major has no symbol, the name is assumed. Any chord written with a plain letter; E, G, C, etc. is a major chord. Sharps and flats make no difference if a chord is major or not, they just raise and lower a chord on the fret board. G, G#, and Gb are *all* major chords, just on different frets. (Review the type I/II chart at the beginning of the book if you need to.) Next up in the chord building cycle are the seventh chords, which add another note to the triad.

60   CHORDS: CHAPTER ONE: CHORD THEORY

7TH CHORDS

NAME	DEGREE FORMULA	STANDARD ABBREVIATION/ PRO SYMBOL
C MAJOR 7	⎡1 3 5⎤ 7 *	C Maj7 / C△7
C MINOR 7	⎡1 b3 5⎤ b7	C min7 / C-7
C DOMINANT 7	⎡1 3 5⎤ b7	C7 / C7
C DIMINISHED 7	⎡1 b3 b5⎤ bb7	C dim7 / C°7
C HALF-DIMINISHED 7	⎡1 b3 b5⎤ b7	Cmin7b5 / Cø7

*basic triads are bracketed

Most guitar players don't realize there are five different types of seventh chords, or that *none* can be substituted for each other! They just play whatever seventh chord form they know and are shocked when it sucks half the time. Notice that all seventh chords contain four notes and are built on top of a triad. Major and dominant sevenths are built over a major triad, minor sevenths over a minor triad, and both diminished seventh chords are built over a diminished triad. (What happened to the augmented triad? That will be explained at the end of the chapter, if you care.) If you don't know how to play a particular seventh chord, don't guess! Just play the triad it's built on, at least you'll have the basics right. Also that bb7 in the diminished chord is not a mistake! You actually have to flat the seventh note twice, which makes it the same as the sixth note. In this case B would be flatted twice to A. Why can't we call it an A? Because we're in chord land! Looking at the abbreviations we continue the same system, with the main differences being the number 7, which tells us to make a four note chord, and the dominant seventh which is assumed for seventh chords. (All chords with a plain 7; C7, E7, B7, etc., are dominant sevenths.)

This concludes the main part of chord theory. If you know the two main premises and have the nine chord names, formulas, and abbreviations down you can work out almost anything with some effort. The reason you need to know these chord formulas is that nothing in the chord name suggests the exact formula used to make it. How would you know to use a major triad and a flat seventh to make a dominant seventh chord? You don't, unless you have even more theory down. Again you really don't even have to know this to play chords by position. However, you do at least have to understand the chord names and abbreviations. If you don't understand the difference between a C7 and a Cmaj7 you are in trouble. I'm finishing this part by demonstrating exactly how to work out more complex chords using our base knowledge. The next level of chords are called natural tensions.

TENSIONS

NATURAL TENSIONS

NAME	DEGREE FORMULA	STANDARD ABBREVIATION/ PRO SYMBOL
MAJOR 9	MAJOR 7 & 9	Maj 9 / △9
MINOR 9	MINOR 7 & 9	min 9 / -9
DOMINANT 9	DOMINANT 7 & 9	9 / 9
MAJOR 11	MAJOR 7 & 9 & 11	Maj 11 / △11
MINOR 11	MINOR 7 & 9 & 11	min 11 / -11
DOMINANT 11	DOMINANT 7 & 9 & 11	11 / 11
MAJOR 13	MAJOR 7 & 9 & 11 & 13	Maj 13 / △13
MINOR 13	MINOR 7 & 9 & 11 & 13	min 13 / -13
DOMINANT 13	DOMINANT 7 & 9 & 11 & 13	13 / 13

Get the idea? All 9s, 11s, and 13s are built on top of three seventh chords. You don't have to alter any more notes (that's why they're called natural), and they are abbreviated the same way. The higher numbers just tell how far up the cycle of thirds you are going. What happened to the diminished sevenths? I'm glad you asked! (It's at the end of this chapter.) What happens if they start changing things? Don't worry, those chords just have altered tensions.

ALTERED TENSIONS

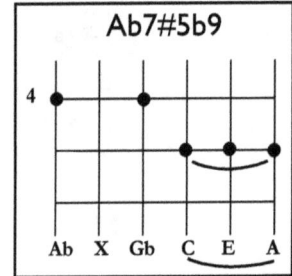

These chords have the scariest looking names, take up the most space in chord books, and are the hardest to use. Other than that, they are fantastic! Seriously, this is where it pays to know chord theory. Lets take that Ab7#5b9 *(see example to the left)* I keep threatening you with. That name is telling me three things:

$$\underset{Ab7}{1} \quad \underset{\#5}{2} \quad \underset{b9}{3}$$

1. Play an Ab7 chord. I just use the dominant seventh chord formula; 1 3 5 b7 with an Ab scale to get the notes Ab C Eb Gb. Check the key of Ab in the appendix if you have to.
2. Sharp the five (#5). The Eb goes up to E.
3. Add a b9. A seventh chord doesn't come with a nine tension, so I need to add one and make it flat as well. In the key of Ab the ninth note is Bb, (same as the second), and I have to flat that, to make Bbb, the same as A. So in this chord I play;

1   3   #5   b7   b9   =   Ab   C   E   Gb   A (Bbb)

See? All that stuff does mean something! Also, if I know chord theory, I can simplify it. Those first three notes, 1 3 #5, look like an augmented triad. That would work OK. This brings up another advantage of knowing chord theory; chords are more of a sound spectrum than a single chord. A Major 9 chord could be simplified all the way down to a simple Major chord, or expanded to a Major 13. You can play around with this concept forever, you're not going to blow up your guitar! So altered tensions are just a list, got it? Hang on, there are only two more concepts to go.

ADDED TENSIONS

I call this the garbage can of the chord world. Sometimes you may want to add a tension, but not go through that whole building in thirds thing. What can you do? Add it! You can add anything, (that's why I call them the garbage can).

C add 9 means play a C and add a 9: $\overline{1\ 3\ 5}$ & 9 = C E G D

Cmin add 11 means play a C minor and add an 11: $\overline{1\ b3\ 5}$ & 11 = C Eb G F

C6 or Cmin6 just means to add a sixth to those chords, etc.

I'm not getting a headache trying to understand this, it's easy!

SUSPENSIONS

There are two suspensions;

NAME	DEGREE FORMULA	STANDARD ABBREVIATION/ PRO SYMBOL
SUSPENDED 2	1 2 5 / C D G	sus2
SUSPENDED 4	1 4 5 / C F G	sus4

This is the only time you mess with a triad. Basically you take out the third and substitute a second or fourth degree. When you take away the third you suspend the normal harmony. That chord is no longer major or minor, so you can use it in place of either. In classical music it's supposed to resolve back to the original chord, but in modern music you don't have to. You may occasionally see a more complex chord, eg. C7sus4, or D9sus4, but all you do is take out the third and substitute the fourth, along with whatever chord you're playing.

The End

Congratulations, you made it! I realize this is a lot to take in and your brain probably hurts, so remember the most important part; *You only have to know the abbreviations!* As long as you know what the name is telling you to do, and you can play the chord forms listed in the next chapter, you will be able to play over a thousand chords! You can always get the rest down later. The final two items in this section are completely optional, but they do explain two questions you may still have. And I *did* promise to answer...

1. What happened to the augmented and diminished chords?
2. How can I play a thirteenth chord with only four fingers and six strings?

OPTIONAL STUFF

Symmetrical Chords

Both augmented and diminished chord formulas are *symmetrical*. For our purposes this just means the notes are the same distance apart. This limits the number of chords you can make, for instance you can *only* make a C augmented triad. Look at the example on the left.

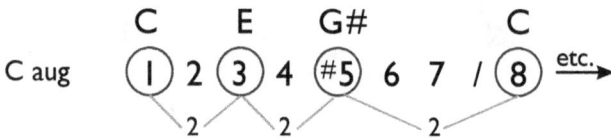

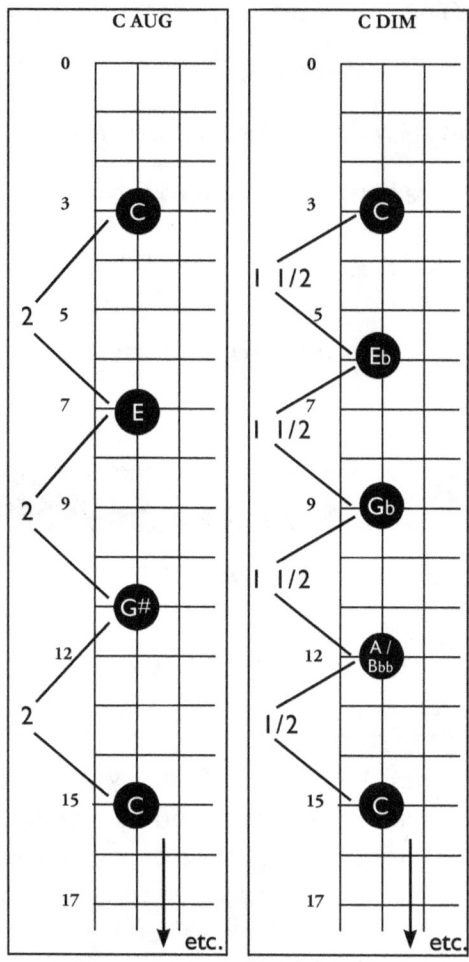

See the problem? The notes in an augmented triad are two whole steps apart, or four frets. By the time you get to the sharp five (G#), you are eight frets from your root (C). If you keep going with this augmented/2 whole step pattern, the next note is four frets higher, a C! We've covered twelve frets and we're back where we started. If we keep building in this augmented/2 whole step pattern, we just keep playing the same three notes. You can't make an augmented seventh chord!* Diminished chords have the same limitations, just with one more note. Look at the example on the right.

This time the notes are one and a half steps, or three frets apart. By the time you get to the double flatted seventh, you are nine frets from your root (C). If you keep going with this diminished/1 1/2 step pattern, the next note is three frets higher, and you are back to the root again. You can't go beyond diminished seventh chords.

That's what happened to the augmented and diminished chords.

If you do find an aug7, it means a dom.7#5, it's not commonly written this way because it's not very clear.

HIERARCHY OF IMPORTANCE

I think I made this term up. It just means that when you make a chord, some notes are more important than others. You really can't play a full thirteenth chord on guitar, because they have seven notes! Only a two-handed keyboard player can do that. What you can do is play the most important notes and leave out the rest. That way you can get the main chord sound without killing yourself. This is how I rank them, from most important to least;

- 1 (the root): Kind of hard to play a C chord without a C! Jazz players will leave out the root for complex chords, because that's the bass players' job. I'm assuming no bass player.
- Third: Normal or flatted, it gives the chord its main character.
- Seventh/highest tension (tie): They're both important. For a thirteenth chord I'd play both notes.
- Altered notes: Any #/b 5's, 9's, etc.
- What's left: Do I have any fingers or strings left? Do I care?

This is how I use this to play a C13:

The total notes in a C13 chord: 1 3 5 b7 9 11 13 = C E G Bb D F A

Out of these seven notes, I chose four: 1 3 b7 13 = C E Bb A

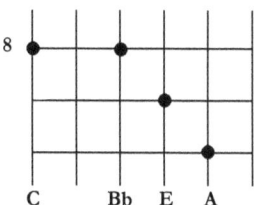

There weren't any altered notes, and nothing else was worth the trouble. If it was a C13b9, I probably would add the flat nine, maybe not. It sounds nasty and it's awkward, so I might blow it off and play either a C7b9 or C13. Voicing complex forms on guitar often involves using your own judgement, that's where the art comes in. A note to all you rock players: Complex chords often sound horrible with distortion. Simplifying them helps, even down to two or three notes. At this level you are suggesting a chord more than playing it, but it beats sounding like garbage. Here's an example:

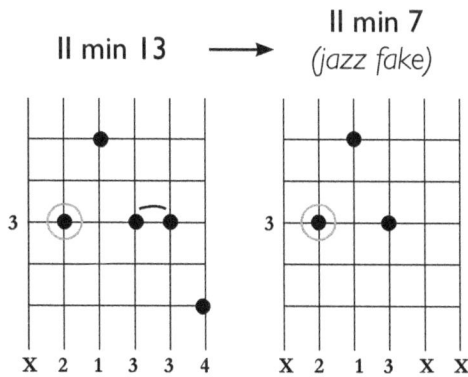

CHORDS: CHAPTER ONE: CHORD THEORY

CHAPTER TWO
Chord Forms

All our talents increase in the using, and every faculty both good and bad, strengthens by exercise.

-Anne Bronte

This section is split into two parts. The first part contains common versions of the basic triads and seventh chords that were covered in the previous section. You probably know some of these already, they are common in popular music; rock, blues, country, pop, etc. The four triads and five seventh chords total up to nine forms in both type I and II versions. The second part contains what I call the Three Jazz Fakes. These simple chords serve as a base to build whatever complex chord you need, and they also allow you to "fake it" in case you can't be bothered! Finally, I've included the two suspended chord forms, just in case. Alert readers will notice that there are a total of fourteen forms, (in both type I and II), which are more than necessary. That's because in some cases I am either showing duplicate ways to play the same chord, or in the case of diminished and augmented triads, showing you chords that almost never get played. Basically I'm either giving you more options, or covering my butt.

TRIADS

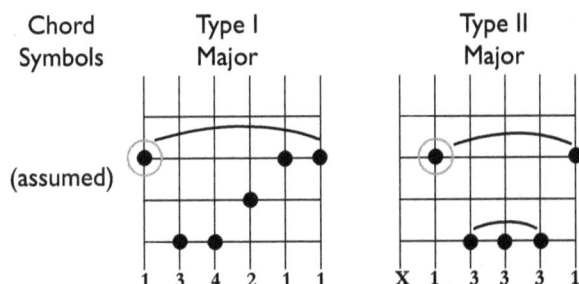

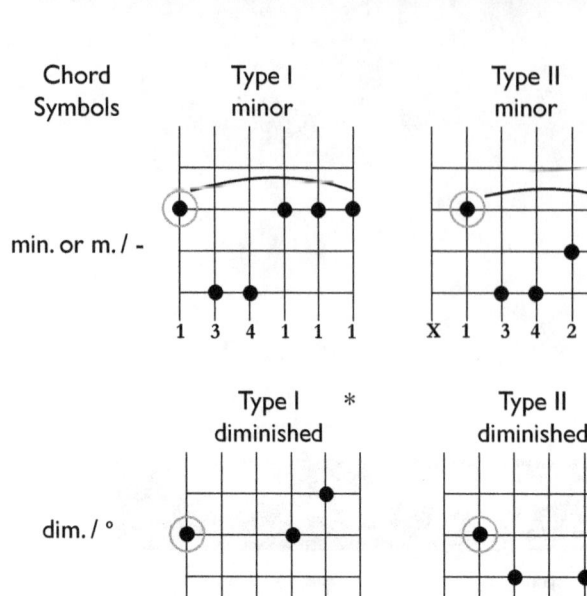

* Play only the strings that you press down with the left hand, mute out the others (X), or don't strum them. Don't whang away on everything!

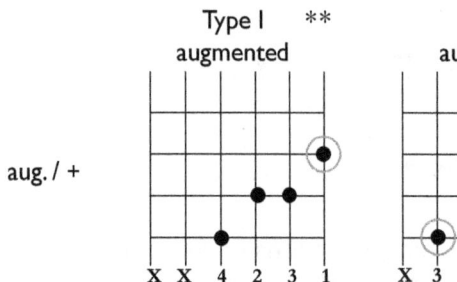

** I consider any chord named off the first string root to be a type I chord, since they share the same notes as the sixth string.

7TH CHORDS

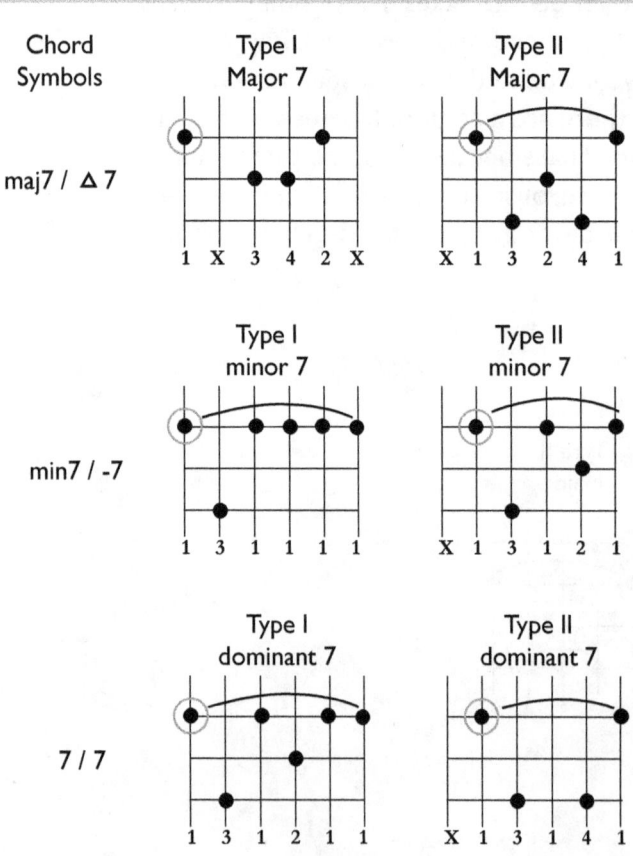

68 CHORDS: CHAPTER TWO: CHORD FORMS

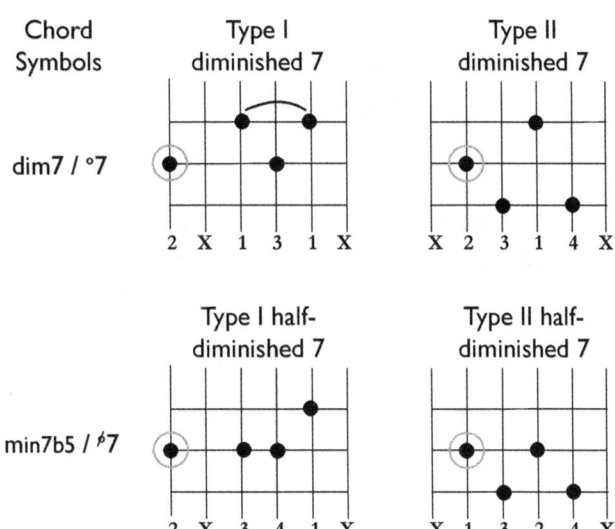

JAZZ FAKES

I came up with this concept when I was coaching a kid having trouble in his high school jazz band. He was a competent rock player, but the constant diet of jazz standards was overwhelming. He was frantically looking in his chord book, trying to memorize dozens of chord forms and alterations. The band director wasn't happy and the kid was stressed. This was a job for Chordmonster! I told my student the band leader really didn't care if he played a perfect chord, he just didn't want any obvious bloopers. If we lowered the bar from "total perfection" to "not obviously blowing it", I could solve his problem with six chord forms! Here they are:

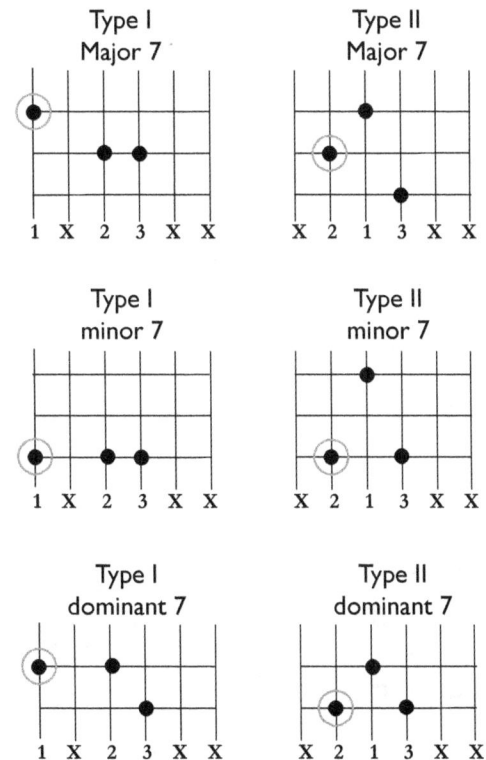

CHORDS: CHAPTER TWO: CHORD FORMS 69

The alert reader will notice that I am repeating myself. You already have these chord types in the first part. What makes these forms special is the other thing you may have noticed, they all contain only three notes. Since a seventh chord, by definition, contains four notes I must have left something out and I did! I left out the fifth. All of these chords contain the root, third and seventh only. In chord theory we saw that all chords exist along a spectrum, from simple to complex. Even a thirteenth chord is basically just a seventh chord with a few extra notes added. So just ignore them! Major 13? Play a jazz fake major 7. Minor 11? Play a jazz fake minor 7. Dominant 9? Play a jazz fake dominant 7. What about alterations? all the #9s and b5s, etc. Ignore them! That's why I left out the fifth, #5?b5?, who cares! You don't even have a five! That scary Ab7#5b9? Play a jazz fake Ab7 instead, it works because you don't care! You aren't playing that complicated alterations/additions game, just the basics and no more! A lot of people think the fakes sound better, after all the more complicated a chord is the weirder it sounds to most people. Basically, I told the kid to ignore any fancy stuff and play the fakes. Major anything, play a major7 fake. Minor anything, play a minor7 fake, etc. Take this example;

simplifies to jazz fake

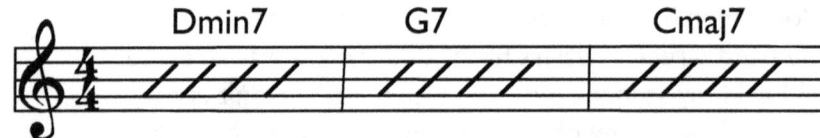

Anyway, the story has a happy ending. (Obviously, or I wouldn't tell it.) The band director was happy and I taught the kid how to easily add those extra tensions and alterations anyway, just like you will in the next part. (I did show the kid how to play a diminished 7, they're hard to fake!) What about 6ths? Play a major. Augmented? How many of those will you see? Play a dominant 7th if you can't ignore it. Missing alterations or tensions? Let the keyboards and the horns worry about it! This is slacker jazz!

ALTERATIONS AND TENSIONS

Modifying jazz fakes is easy. You can find whatever notes you might need close by the basic form, and more importantly, *in the same relative location!* Look at the following diagrams which contain only the alterations and tensions for type I and II fakes.

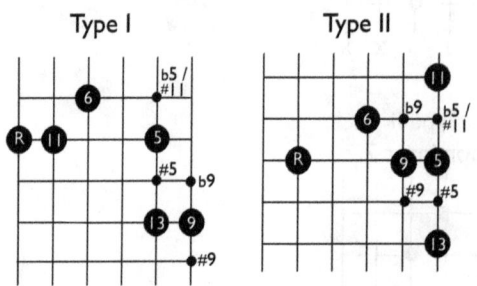

* Astute readers will notice that you have to remove a note from the jazz fake in order to add a 6th. This works out fine since you are removing the seventh degree in all cases (which is not in a 6th chord anyway).

To make this absolutely clear, here are all six jazz fakes with the tensions and alterations added.

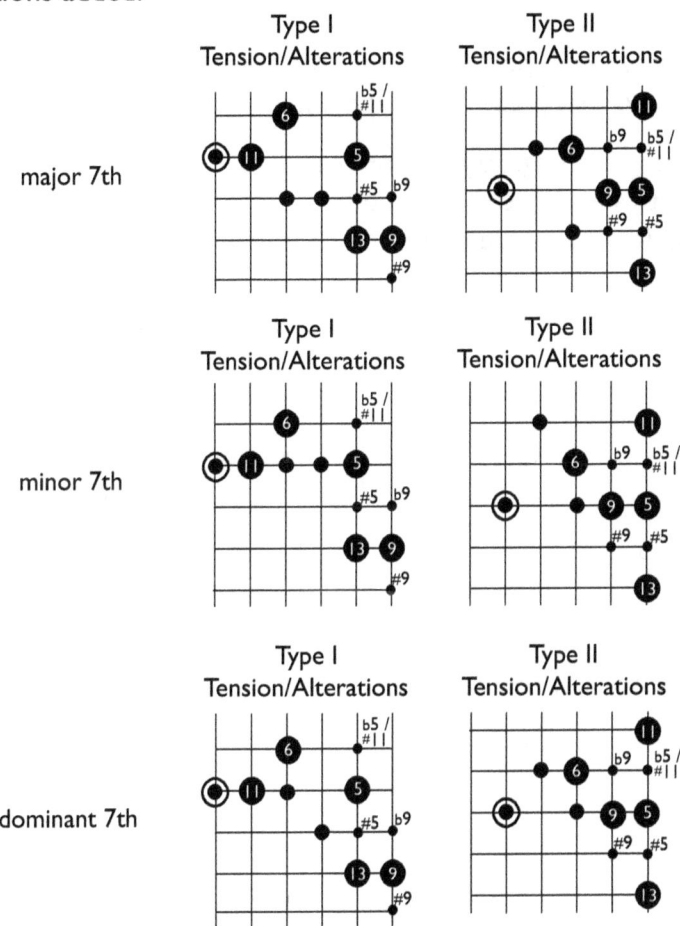

A sharp five is the same for any type I chord, (or type II). Major 7, minor 7, or dominant 7, just plug in the basic form! Below are the three Type I chords.

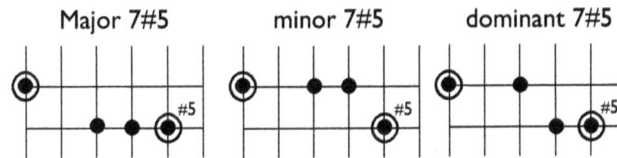

You can combine these alterations at least twelve different ways! (I've listed fifteen possibilities below.) Since some combinations can be either nonsensical or impossible to play, I am conservatively estimating twelve additions/alterations for each fake type.

6 | 7#5 | 7b5 | 9 | 7b9 | 7#9 | 7b5b9 | 7b5#9 | 7#5#9

7#5b9 | 11 | 11#5 | 11b9 | 13 | 13b9

There are two cautions:

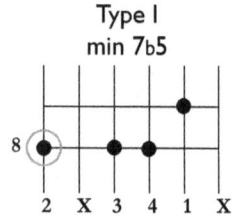
Type II min 7b5

- Everything has a price. Some types/alterations are pretty awkward or don't sound that great, like a type II minor7b5.
- You will have to adjust your fingering for some altered chords. For instance, this example would require you to adjust your fingers unless you were extremely flexible.

You have three alternative choices;

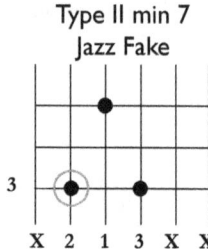
Type I min 7b5

- Play the other type.

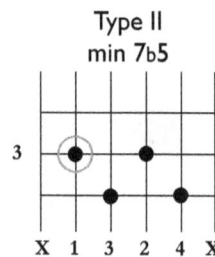
Type II min 7 Jazz Fake

- Play the jazz fake, and don't worry about it.

Type II min 7b5

- If you encounter the chord a lot, or you just can't take it, drag out your chord book/app and look it up.

72   **CHORDS:** CHAPTER TWO: CHORD FORMS

SUSPENSIONS

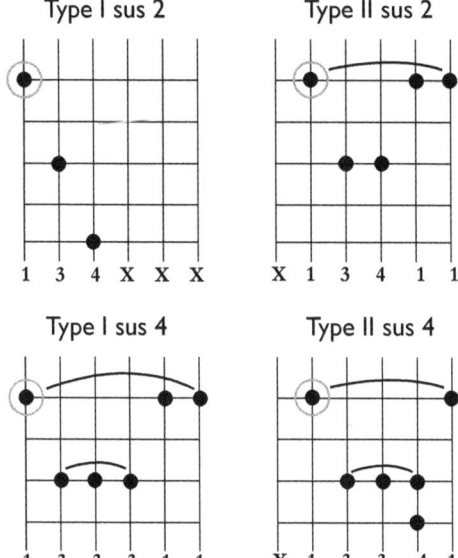

Suspended chords are used quite a lot in all forms of popular music. They are worth learning, even for the lazy!

Chapter Two Summary:

Read em and weep. In this chapter, I have shown fourteen chord forms for both type I and type II for a total of twenty eight forms! Quit whining and consider the following;

- You probably already know some of these forms.
- Counting all of the possibilities; I/II roots, twelve different root notes, duplications and alterations of the fakes, you can play approximately one thousand two hundred chords!* True some chords might be awkward to play or not sound that great, but that's true for any chord dictionary. Learning twenty eight forms is a hassle, but learning twelve hundred chords is impossible.
- *The math for my claim:
  - 14 basic forms with no alterations (includes fakes and suspensions)
  - Add 12 alterations for each of the three jazz fakes (for a total of 36 possible chords)
  - The 50 forms (14+36 above) on all 12 frets brings us to 600 chords.
  - Finally with both type I and type II, we double the number to 1200 chords.
- If twelve hundred chords isn't enough, you can read the name of any chord and work it out. Figure the notes first, using the chord name, then either fake it or locate the notes on your guitar and work out a fingering. Use the hierarchy to simplify, if needed.
- If all else fails you can fake everything with six type I/II forms, for a total of twelve. This is in the final summary.

SCALES

CHAPTER ONE
The Basics

Rests always sound well.
    -Arnold Schoenberg

If you only know one scale, make it a *pentatonic** scale. In my opinion, it's the most versatile scale and you can use it for all popular styles. It's also the foundation of both *major* and *blues scales*, which are the other two scales commonly used in popular music. A pentatonic scale is easy to play, easy to use, and hard to screw up, and did I mention it works over just about anything? Yes I did! Here is the most common pentatonic position, which many of you probably know:

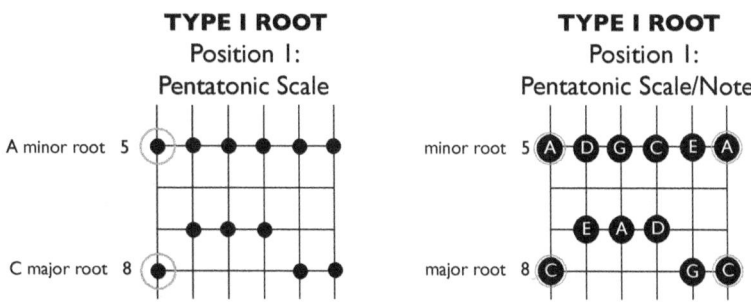

Everybody knows this position. It's the easiest position to play and it's the most used. Almost half of all guitar solos I have ever figured out in forty years of playing and teaching guitar have been in this single position. This is the first position I try when I'm learning a new solo and many famous players have built careers on this position, and not much else. For this reason, this is commonly called position one, because there are four more positions to learn if you want to play the entire neck. But you *don't* have to learn them all! You can be a GOOD GUITARIST with this one position, in fact, why be in a rush? Learn how to use this position before you learn the rest.

The first step in using this scale is figuring out what key you want to play in. This is easy, since a first position pentatonic scale has the same root as a type I bar chord. Or two roots, to be precise. Notice the top (8th fret) note of the position is the major root, and the bottom (5th fret) note is the minor root.

*Pentatonic means five notes, because the scale contains only five notes repeated indefinitely! Look at the example on the right, above.

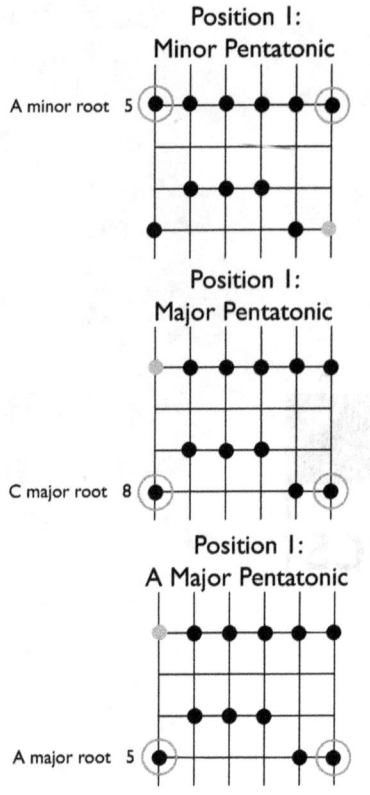

As we learned in the mode lesson, major and minor are just different ways to play the same scale. If you want a minor scale, play from the minor root (top example), play from the major root for a major scale (middle example). This one position is both C major and A minor, depending on the root. This is called relative major and minor, it's the same scale played from two different roots or modes. What if you want an A major? Move the position down and put the top note on fret five, (bottom example) now you're playing an A major! (and an F#minor). It's two scales in one, get the picture? Top note major, bottom note minor.

You can play whatever key you want, just locate the type 1 root, put down the correct finger, and play! For example, do you want to play a...

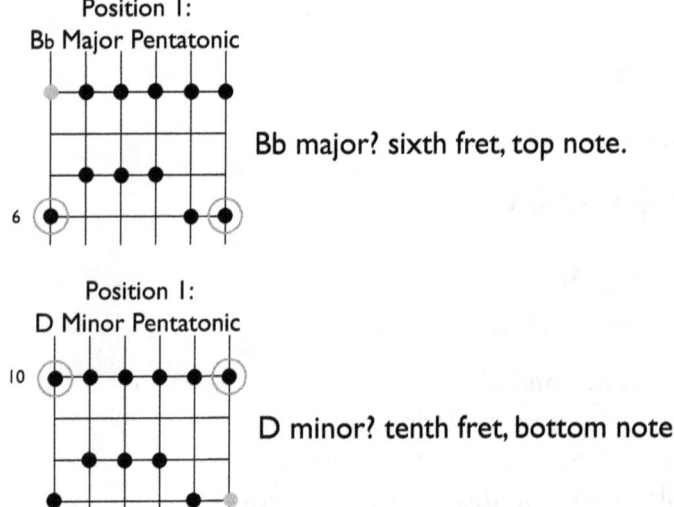

Bb major? sixth fret, top note.

D minor? tenth fret, bottom note.

Once you're in the correct key you can play anywhere in the scale, you don't have to always start on the root. Now you have only one challenge left: What the hell do you play?

78 SCALES: CHAPTER ONE: THE BASICS

HOW TO USE THE SCALE

Face it, you don't need this book to learn scales. You can learn hundreds on-line for free. The problem is what to do with them. Playing a scale does not transform you into a lead guitarist! Fear not, over the years I developed a simple metaphor that explains how to do that. Are you ready? Are you sitting down? Good, here it is: Learning how to play lead guitar is like learning how to read. Can you do that? Probably so. Are you impressed with my metaphor? Probably not, but give it a chance. You learned to read in three stages, and you will become a lead guitarist in three stages that are very similar.

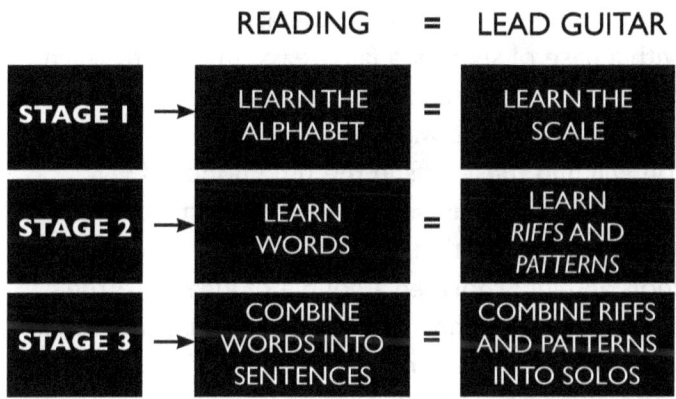

- In stage one, learning a scale is like learning your ABC's. The only thing a scale does is tell you what notes you can play, not what to do with them. You can't do much reciting the alphabet either, it's kind of boring, like playing a scale! But it is the foundation in both cases, you have to learn it first.

- When you began to read in the second stage, you combined a few letters together to form words. In music you combine a few notes together to form *riffs*, or play repeating sequences of notes called *patterns*. Simply put, a riff is a few notes that sound good together. How many is "a few"? Generally about three to six, the longer a riff is the less versatile, so much more than six notes is pushing it. The "official" name for a riff is *melodic motif*! The next time you want to compliment a guitar player, tell them you admire their selection of melodic motifs, and see if they punch you out! What determines if a riff sounds good? You do! Rock riffs, blues riffs, country riffs, even jazz riffs are all possible with notes from a pentatonic scale. I may like a particular riff and you may hate it. Play riffs you like, not what somebody tells you to like!

Scale patterns are simple, (2-6 note) note sequences that repeat in specific rhythms. They can move up and down the neck without changing, because they're patterns! Patterns are more mechanical, (a triplet pattern sounds the same whether Bach does it or Jimmy Page), but they are useful! This brings up a crucial difference between riffs and patterns;

Riffs generally don't move; they are made from a specific group of notes. *(next section)*

Patterns move; since they are repeating sequences of notes, you can play them on just two strings, or across all six strings and between several positions. *(next section)*

- The fun begins in the third stage, when you start combining things. When you are learning to read you combine words together and form sentences. Finally you can read something! When you are learning lead guitar you combine riffs and patterns together and play solos. Finally you can play a solo! In my little analogy; the scale is the alphabet, riffs and patterns are the vocabulary, and solos are sentences (long solos are paragraphs!). Therefore it would seem that the more riffs and patterns you know, the better solos you can play because you have a larger "vocabulary". Generally speaking this is true, but you can become quite a decent lead guitarist with very few riffs. This because unlike words in sentences, riffs in solos have no *syntax*. There are no subject riffs or verb riffs, etc., you can combine riffs and patterns any way you want! In it's most basic state, a solo is just a collection of riffs and patterns, the art is in how well you do it! I would suggest starting with a base of six riffs, a fairly easy amount to learn. Later on in this section, I will give you a list of six generic riffs you can use for rock, blues, etc., but this will only be for demonstration. You want riffs you like, not bland generic stuff everybody else plays! You will find these riffs in the time honored way that everybody else has, you will steal them from your heroes! *Everybody* starts this way, even your heroes stole riffs from their heroes! It's a perfectly natural process, they copied a few solos from their idols and incorporated a couple of ideas into their playing style. Don't call it stealing, call it influence! When you hear a guitarist say, "I was heavily influenced by BB King", it means, "I stole a lot of riffs from BB King". That's OK, because even BB King didn't invent everything he played. Everybody does it! We're just going to do it a little more systematically.

YOUR SIX RIFFS

I always start by asking my students who their top three lead guitarists are. Then I ask them to pick a favorite solo from each. The final step is to learn each solo, not just how to play it, but what key it's in, the scale positions used, everything! Then we pick two riffs from each solo and practice those riffs in all twelve keys, using whatever scale position the riff was in. Here is the basic idea:

Guitarist 1	Solo	2 Riffs
Guitarist 2	Solo	2 Riffs
Guitarist 3	Solo	2 Riffs

At the end of this process they know three different solos by their favorite players, and more important, have a collection of six riffs nobody else has! I can ask a thousand players who their favorite players are and get about a thousand different answers. Even if players share the same three guitarists, they don't pick the same solos and certainly not the same riffs! Therefore each player will wind up with a unique set of six riffs that reflect *their* particular likes, and nobody else will have those exact riffs! Along with a scale pattern or two, these six riffs will be the foundation of *your* soloing style. How do you turn six riffs and a couple of patterns into a good sounding solo style? By jamming! Learning to solo is like learning to ride a bike; at first your solos sound like clumsily strung together riffs, but the more you do it the smoother you get! There is a section on jamming in the appendix, but I would like to finish up this section by answering a few questions I generally get.

What if I only like two guitarists? Or one? Does it have to be all guitarists?

Obviously three is an arbitrary number, for both guitarists and solos. The only fixed number for now is six riffs. Split it up however you like; get all six riffs from one solo if you want! But if you have only one influence, guess who you're going to sound like! There's a difference between influences and being a copycat. Getting riffs from other instruments is a great idea, if you can figure them out and play them. It will allow you to sound more original, since you're not using the same guitar riffs everyone else is. In fact if you could find a few obscure horn players from fifty years ago, and get some riffs from them, people might think you're a creative genius!

What can I do with only six riffs?

Quite a lot, actually. This is because as I said in a previous paragraph, you can combine riffs anyway you want. So how many ways can you mix up six riffs? If you consider a solo to be some combination of six riffs, you can factor it out; $6 \times 5 \times 4 \times 3 \times 2 \times 1 = 720$ combinations! That's just playing them each one time. This doesn't count playing patterns, rhythmic variations, or playing a riff twice! I realize this is only what is possible mathematically, many of the combinations may not sound that good. But even ten percent is 72 solos! That's why these six core riffs are important, they will always be a part of your sound. Even though you will learn more riffs and maybe make up a few of your own, you can always go back to your basic six. In my opinion, this is one reason for any guitarist's sound. If you listen to enough of their solos, you will hear them repeating riffs!

This sounds too mechanical, where's the art?

True improvisation happens when you can play what you hear in your mind. This will begin to happen as you internalize your scales. Playing a lot helps, so does singing along with your scales and riffs, matching them exactly. Still, there are worse things than being a little mechanical when you play. Like incompetence. Many guitarists never get past the riff stage of playing and do just dandy. Even when you can play what you hear, what if you draw a blank during your solo? Out come the riffs.

How do I figure out these solos?

I generally figure out the solos for my students, but I'm not here! Figuring out solos, especially the good ones, on your own is tough. It takes a while to learn that skill, and many players never do. Although I have a short section on song/solo transcription in the Theory Summary chapter, I doubt it will turn you into an instant pro! Therefore you can use commercially available tabs, YouTube videos, guitar transcription software (like Guitar Pro & their library), or bust up and find somebody like myself who can listen to music and transcribe it. If there is an "official tab transcription" available, I would buy it. Do not waste your time on somebody's free tab, you're putting in too much effort! Whichever way you learn, figure out the scale position and the key they're playing your riff in, so you can play it in all twelve keys.

Chapter One Summary:

Now that you can locate and play a simple pentatonic scale position in both major and minor keys, and you've got my basic lead solo philosophy, it's time to move on. The next section will show you how to actually use the scale and put this philosophy in action!

CHAPTER TWO
Using the Scale

The shortest answer is doing.
-English proverb

This section is focused on the application of the ideas presented in the first section. For the sake of illustration, I will show a *triplet pattern* and six generic riffs, plus a few examples of combining them in a solo. Both the pattern and the riffs will be written in *tablature*. If you're not clear on how to read tablature, or the abbreviations I use for performance, check the tablature section in the appendix. Since all riffs and patterns in this section will be played on position 1 pentatonic scale, I am showing it again for reference.

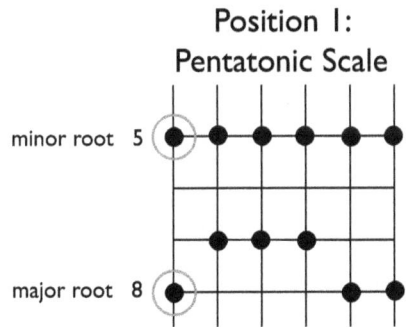

THE TRIPLET PATTERN

This is one of the most commonly used patterns in popular music, because it's simple and works with most styles. Many of my students probably have nightmares about the triplet pattern, since I use this to show them the entire neck! Lucky for you, we are only interested in the first position for now. A note on fingering: This position, like most, occupies four frets of the neck. Use one finger per fret, 1st finger for fret five, 3rd finger for fret seven, 4th finger for fret eight, (there are no 6th fret notes in this position, so you don't use your second finger.) The goal is to play the position and move your hand as little as possible. Let your fingers do the walking!

THE TRIPLET PATTERN: DESCENDING

Track #3

THE TRIPLET PATTERN: ASCENDING

- Notice that in spite of all the notes, you are just playing overlapping groups of three notes non-stop. Hey, maybe that's why they call it a triplet pattern!

- The goal is to play the entire pattern smoothly and evenly, non-stop. Work on eliminating any gaps between triplets. Just accent the first note of each triplet a little, to mark the group of three.

- Although we are playing this pattern across the entire position, this is only for exercise! Normally patterns are used for only two or three strings, just to connect riffs or move to another area of the neck. A pattern is too boring to use for long.

SIX GENERIC RIFFS

Although I trashed generic riffs previously, I actually think they can be quite useful. After all, they became cliches for a reason; they're easy to play, versatile, and give a lot of bang for the buck. Also there are worse things than being generic, like being incompetent. The following six riffs will be useful over most styles of music, and will hold you until you come up with your own ideas.

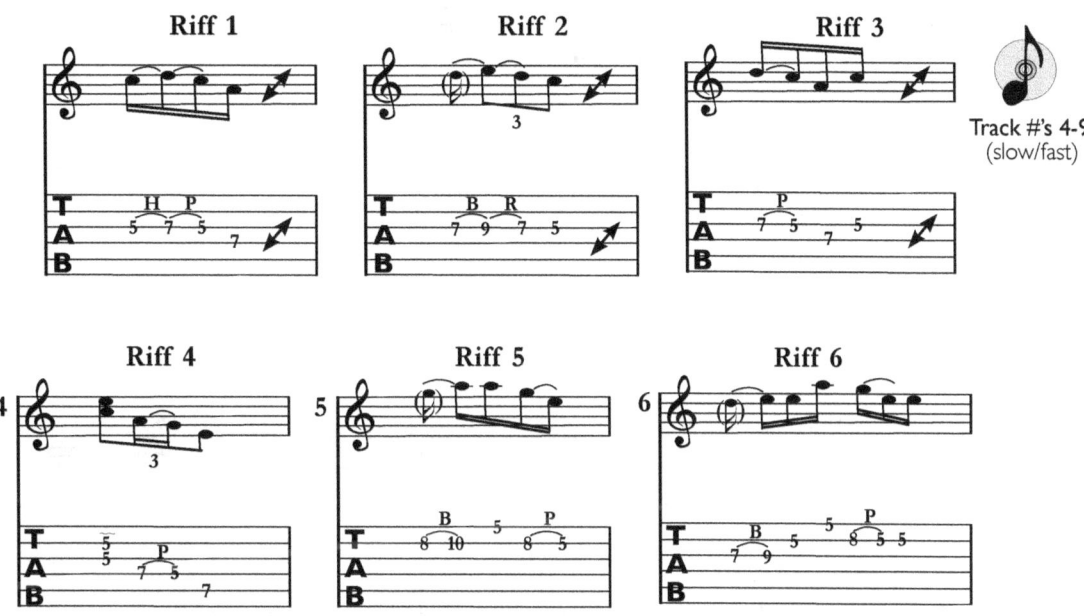

Track #'s 4-9
(slow/fast)

- Notice that all six riffs will work over both C major and A minor, although some will work better than others for a particular mode. Many riffs you may learn will be more specialized and designed for major or minor, but these riffs are generic!

- These riffs can be played at whatever speed you desire, or can manage. Obviously it would be best to learn and practice them slowly at first.

- The top three riffs can be moved to different strings if you adjust for the changing scale notes.

PUTTING IT ALL TOGETHER

I've chosen a simple twelve bar blues to show one possible way to combine these six riffs along with what ever bits of the triplet pattern may come in handy. Although the blues is the best place to start, these riffs will work with rock and country rock solos as well. But in the blues, the tempo is slower and it's easier to play and comprehend. I have identified the riffs by number above the solo, and I have kept any extra notes to a minimum. Please note that this solo is an example, not an artistic expression of my innermost soul! I've made a point to use every riff and the triplet pattern in one verse. In addition, I've kept any rhythmic variations to a minimum to make it easier to play. Any real solo would contain about a third of the riffs, a lot more rhythmic variation, and definitely more empty space between notes. This is just a demo. (In track 11, I play the same solo twice as fast to show how the riffs can be used for rock.)

SCALES: CHAPTER TWO: USING THE SCALE

Chapter Two Summary:

This section illustrates the components of soloing. You have learned: a triplet scale pattern, six generic riffs, and a twelve bar blues solo that uses these elements. Although I chose a twelve bar blues for my solo example, these riffs and patterns are generic and versatile enough to work over both rock and modern country as well. Remember this is for demonstration only, hopefully *you* will pick better riffs!

CHAPTER THREE
More Scales

> Practice yourself, for heavens' sake, in little things; and thence proceed to greater.
>
> -Epictetus

The lead guitarist does not live by the pentatonic scale alone. The reason a pentatonic scale is so easy to play and works over so many different musical styles is because it's basic. In fact, in my view it's a *framework* scale. You may have noticed that while I've covered major, minor and blues keys and scales, I have not mentioned pentatonic keys. That's because the pentatonic scale is a simple scale contained inside those other scales! It acts like a basic frame, if you add a certain group of notes to a pentatonic scale, you get a full major/minor scale. If you add a mostly different group of notes, you get a blues scale. Notice that even though a major scale and a blues scale contain different notes, there is a pentatonic scale inside of each! That's why a pentatonic scale is so versatile, it's the foundation for everything.

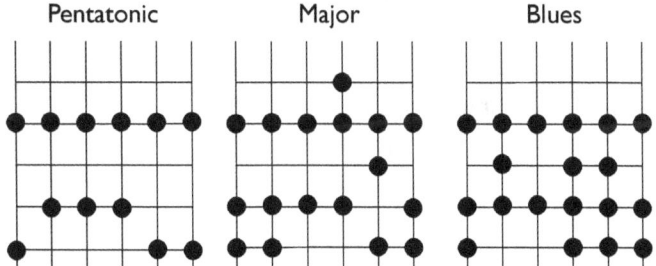

In order to use the major and blues scales effectively, you must know the key you are in. If you are in a blues key and you play a major scale, the results will not sound great. The same goes for playing a blues scale over a major key, mostly barfy! Hopefully you can use your understanding of theory to analyze the chords and determine the key, but trial and error works too. If one scale sounds bad, try the other. If all else fails, play a pentatonic! As long as you're on the right fret, it has to work.

Most guitarists never play all of the extra notes available, especially in a blues scale. They will pick a few extra notes and add them to the pentatonic scale. A complete blues scale has so many notes it sounds dumb played all at once. Think of the extra notes in a blues scale as possibilities, you don't need to use them all. Since a blues scale contains both major and minor notes, only one root is generally used which corresponds to the minor root in a pentatonic. (It is possible to use the major root, but I see this much less often.)

Both pentatonic and major scales share the same roots for major and minor modes.

Finally, always remember the pentatonic scale is your friend! If you aren't sure what kind of key you're in, or you're too tired or drunk to care, play a pentatonic. After all, there are only twelve possible frets to play and it's got to be one of them!

SCALES UP THE NECK

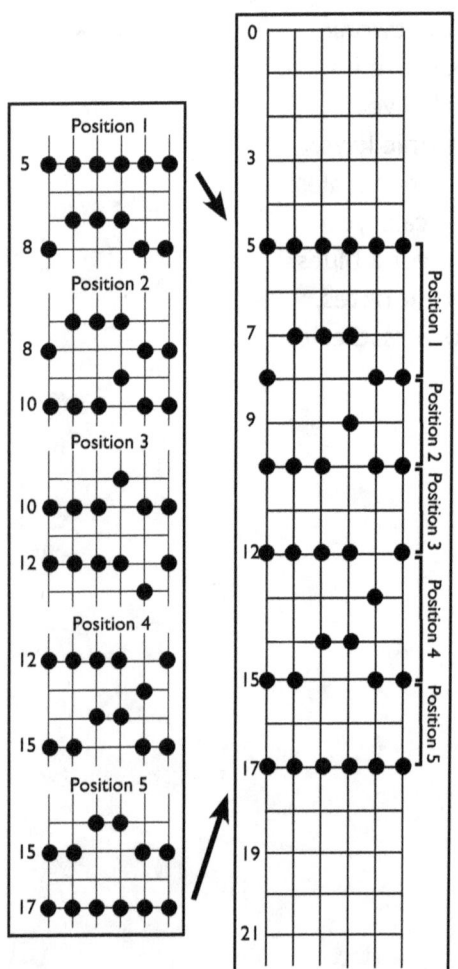

In order to play scales across the entire fret board, you will need to know five scale positions. While you can play in every key with only the first position, (by changing the fret to match the type I root), you are still only playing in a four fret area. With all five positions you can play anywhere on the neck, in any key. The same procedure we used for position one applies to the remaining four positions, ie., a basic pentatonic "frame" scale position is filled in with extra major or blues scale notes. For those of you who are good at math, this means a total of fifteen separate positions! In twelve different keys! Good luck! Obviously this could take a while, but as a wise man (me) said, you eat the elephant one bite at a time. In this case it means starting with the pentatonic scale. The example on the left shows all five positions in the key of C major.

The example on the right shows all five positions together. Notice that the positions all stack on top of one another, the top notes of one position become the bottom notes of the next.

Taken together, these five positions cover twelve frets of the guitar neck, from fret five to fret seventeen. This covers a complete octave, which means the position sequence starts over. You play position one on fret seventeen, etc., until you run out of frets. It's an endless sequence, just keep playing positions one through five (or five through one if you're going down the neck). The next two examples illustrate this.

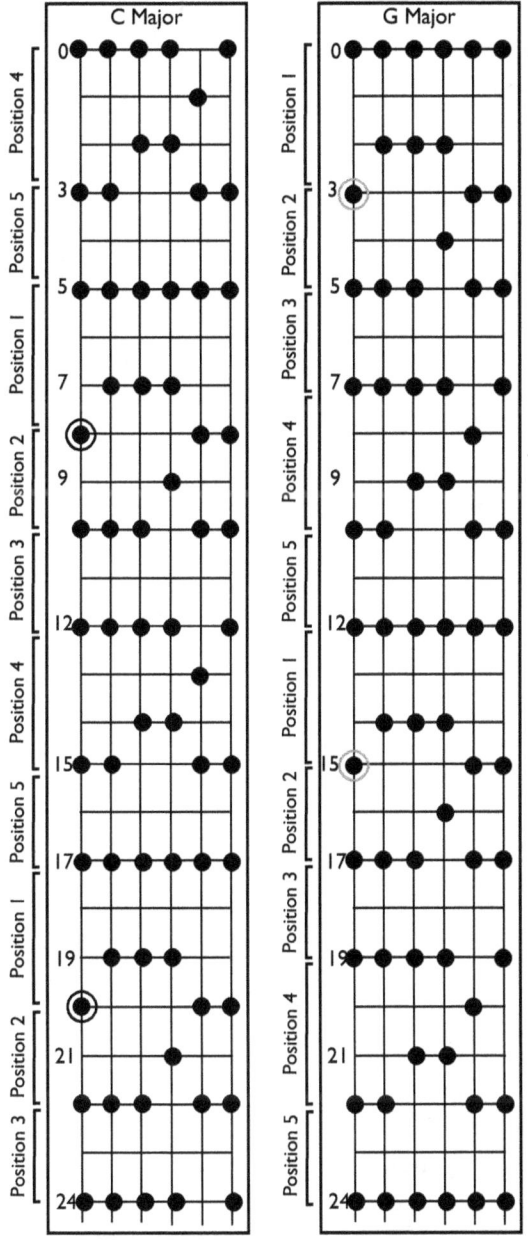

For these examples, I have used a 24 fret neck, but it doesn't matter if you have twenty frets or thirty frets, just keep playing positions one through five. This sequence is the same for all keys, the only difference is where you start position one, with the type 1 root. This means you can play all twelve keys with the same sequence, if you can play one key you can play them all! Here is the key of C major compared with the key of G major.*

Notice the position sequence is the same for both keys, the only difference is the location with the C root on the eighth fret and the G root on fret three.

*Remember C major is also A minor and G major is also E minor.

The next page is the Master Scale Position Chart. This page lays out the three main scales; pentatonic, major/minor, and blues, in all five positions. I have chosen the key of C major/A minor, (and A blues since the blues scale root and the minor root are usually the same), but as I've said earlier the sequence of positions is the same for any key, just start the position sequence on a different type 1 root.

THE MASTER SCALE POSITION CHART

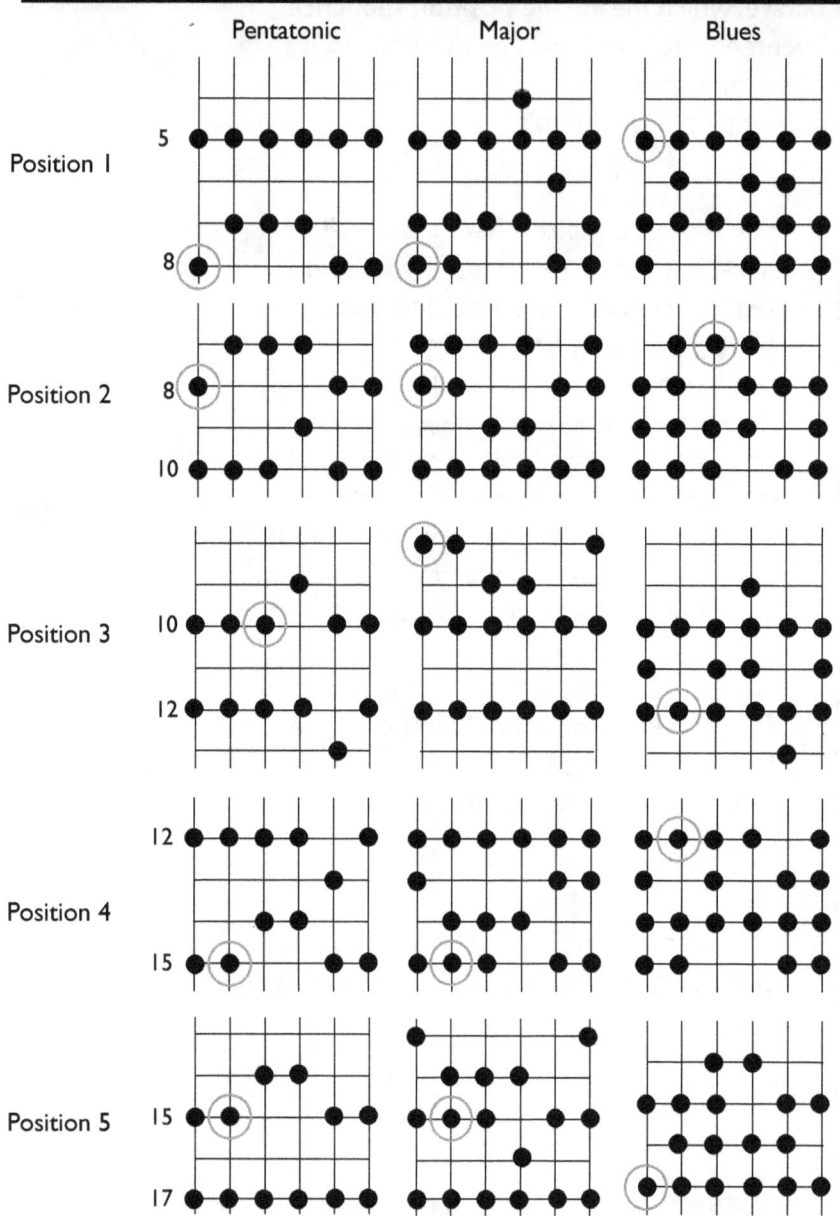

Major roots are circled for pentatonic and major scales, and minor roots are circled for the blues scale.

FINDING YOUR WAY WITH TYPE I/II ROOTS

Confused? You should be, that's a lot of information. It takes years to get this down in all twelve keys, much less develop fast technique. If playing great guitar was easy, everyone would do it. But you don't have to do it all now! Learn position one first and play with it for awhile, then add the major and blues notes and see what sounds good. Learn some riffs and jam! When position one starts to make sense, the next position you might learn is position four. Why skip to position four? Because position four is named from a type II root.

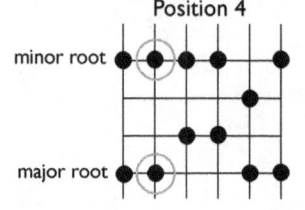

Notice the root locations are the same as type I, just located on the fifth string, instead of the sixth string. (Type I=6th string root, type II=5th string root.)

SCALES: CHAPTER THREE: MORE SCALES

Just knowing these two positions can get you decent coverage (50%) on the neck. For example, if a song was in G minor, I would locate my scale positions to match my chords (shown in the two examples on the left).

The same would work for G major (shown in the two examples on the right). Remember first finger is the minor root and fourth finger is the major root.

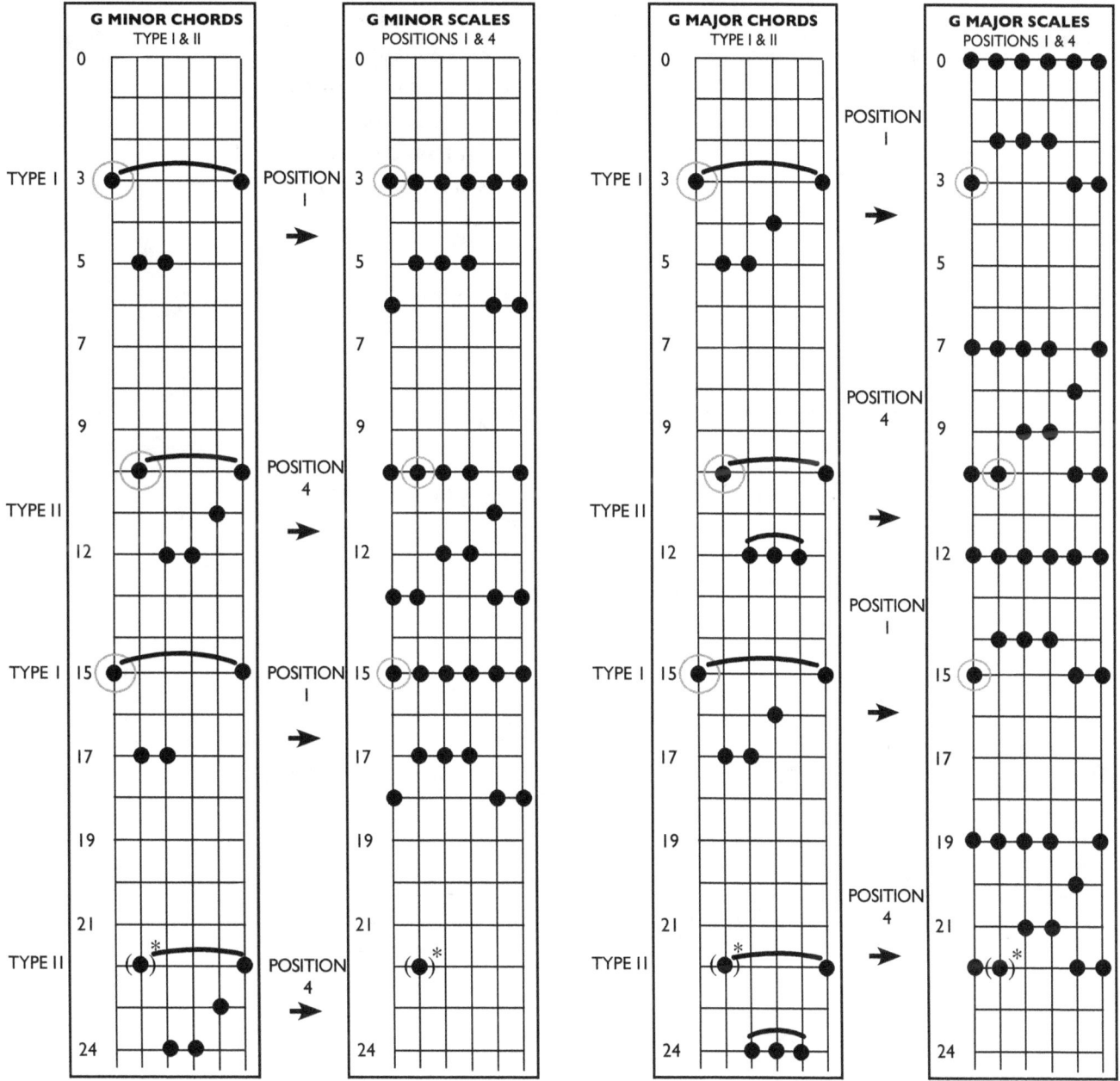

I can locate my scales as fast as my chords! This is why learning your type I and II roots is crucial. You use the same roots for everything. Obviously I don't have to stick with pentatonics. I can fill in the major or blues notes if I want.

Ultimately these two positions can serve as guide posts as you learn more positions. If you get lost, think of the chord and play the scale to match. You can't stay lost for long!

*hard to impossible to play!

USING A SCALE PATTERN TO CONNECT POSITIONS

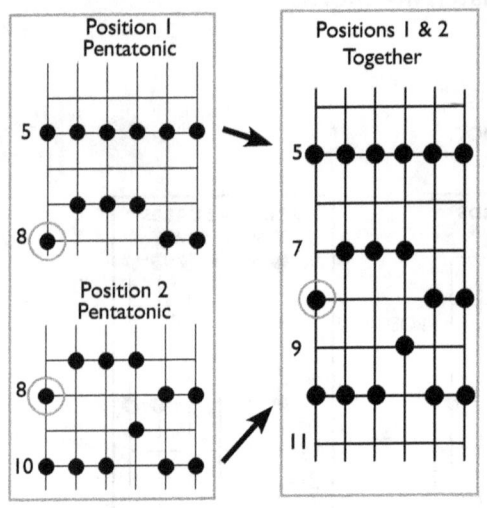

Scale patterns are a handy way to connect scale positions. You can use them to connect riffs (see twelve bar blues solo in Chapter 2), but I also use them to teach my students how to play up and down the neck. You don't have to use a pattern to move between positions! You can slide a note or just jump between positions, whatever you want. Since you don't need lessons on how to do whatever you want, I'm going to demonstrate how to use the triplet pattern to move between positions one and two. Here are the two positions separately and together.

Notice that the two positions share notes. This is always the case with pentatonics.

Before we learn how to connect using a triplet pattern, I would suggest learning how to play the triplet pattern in the second position.

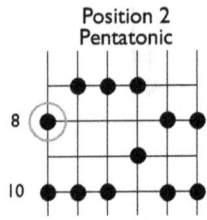

This is the same note sequence as the triplet pattern in position one, just played over a different position shape. This is why patterns are useful, they repeat! When you learn a pattern in one position, transferring it to the next position is a lot easier.

POSITION 2: DESCENDING

POSITION 2: ASCENDING

94 SCALES: CHAPTER THREE: MORE SCALES

CONNECTING POSITIONS 1 & 2

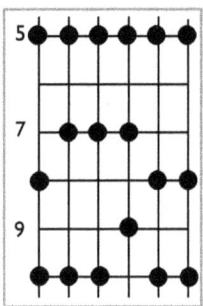

Now that you can play the pattern in both positions (hopefully you reviewed position one), it's time to connect. For the first example, I have connected on the third string. The diagram on the left shows both positions for reference.

CONNECTING STRING 3 DESCENDING

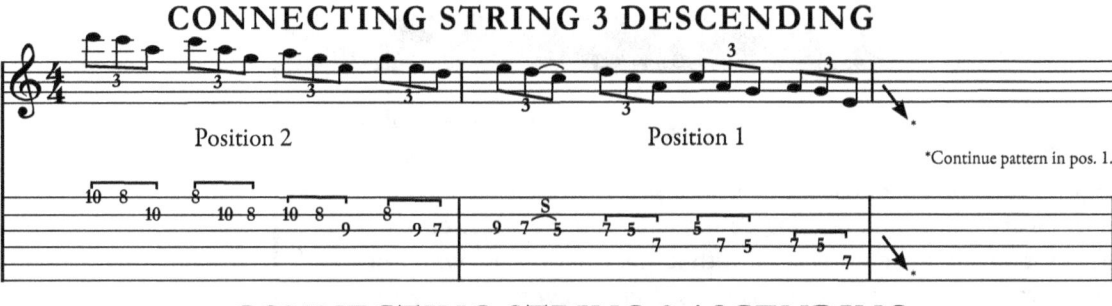

CONNECTING STRING 3 ASCENDING

Pay attention to the actual switching triplet, notated in the second measure. This is how to switch without breaking the pattern.

This same method can be used for any string, and you don't have to switch back and forth on the same string. The next example connects down on the second string and up on the fifth string.

CONNECTING DESCENDING: STRING 2

CONNECTING ASCENDING: STRING 5

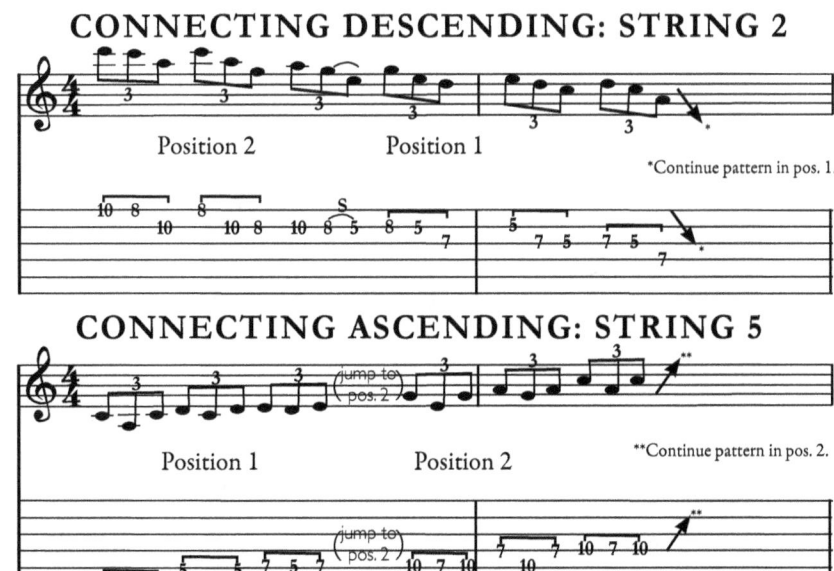

I have my students connect on all six strings, in both directions. That gets the point across!

SCALES: CHAPTER THREE: MORE SCALES

You will notice that the note sequence sounds the same no matter which string you connect on. This is because they are the same! You use patterns to connect riffs, which could be anywhere. If you can only connect on the third string and your riff is on the fifth string, you are out of luck. Being able to move on any string gives a lot more flexibility.

This same connection procedure can be used between any two positions. That's how you learn the neck. After you can connect positions one and two, learn position three and then connect that, and so on...

Chapter Three Summary:

Learning scales can take a long time. It could take several years for these three scales; pentatonic, major/minor, and blues. And I hate to break it to you, but there are more scales, many more. Get a scale book and learn hundreds if you want. But for most popular music, these three are plenty, and burning up the neck is not a requirement. My advice is to learn one position and get comfortable with it. You can do a lot with one position, and many guitarists, including some famous ones, don't know much more. I would say almost half of all the solos I have ever transcribed or played have taken place in position one. Remember, it's better to be very good with a few things than mediocre on a lot of things!

SUMMARY

SUMMARY

> Our life is frittered away by detail. Simplify, simplify.
> -Henry David Thoreau

In the beginning I promised to show you a simple system that worked for most popular music. Through out this book I have explained everything in the form of pictures and located it all using only the two bar chord roots shown in the first chapter. Although I have tried to use real world examples and problems to illustrate these concepts, they have been spread through the text. Therefore in this summary I have two goals; First, to explain in a basic way how you can use this system to take control over a constant barrage of new information and second, how to fit it all on the two pages I promised at the start!

TAKING CONTROL

NEW SONGS: Besides using theory to help figure out a song, you can also unlock information. If you like the chord progression enough to learn it why not figure out the chord degrees and try the same progression in new keys? Whole new songs can be created by combining progressions from two or more songs into new keys.

NEW SOLOS: Any solo should be viewed as a source for riffs. Once you learn all five scale positions, that's it. The entire neck is accounted for no matter how many frets it has. Use your theory knowledge to determine the key (from the chords), and your scale knowledge to determine what positions are being used. (What position shapes are your fingers in when you play the solo?) Then pick your favorite riff and move its' position to other keys, change the tempo, etc. Now you have another riff in your arsenal!

NEW CHORDS: Can you relate it to a type I/II (6th/5th string) root? If the root is on some other string will you be able to move it easily? Does it depend on open strings (which means you are probably limited in movement). If the chord is a one trick pony, is it worth it? Read the name and find another way to play it or simplify it. However some chords are too cool to pass up, so if you have the neurons to spare, why not.

JAMS/ORIGINALS: See new songs and solos above, as well as relevant appendix info. Everybody sounds derivative and clumsy at first. The more songs you write and the more you jam, the better. Find a local open mic night, join a song writers' group, play in church, or find some jamming buddies on the web. Don't be a closet case!

Congratulations! I hope this book has helped you on your journey. Understanding how scales and chords work in all types of music does help to tie it all together. I use this knowledge almost daily to decide what music to learn and how to apply it to the music I already know. The more you know, the more you can take control. Good Luck!

Jim Beckwith

PS, As promised, the following two pages list the absolute minimum to memorize! Get this down and you can play (or fake) all of the chords and lead in any key, with zero theory. You can also "fake" thousands of complex chords with the jazz fakes (as long as you can read the chord name).

I may have faults but being wrong ain't one of them.
-Jimmy Hoffa

THE ABSOLUTE MINIMUM

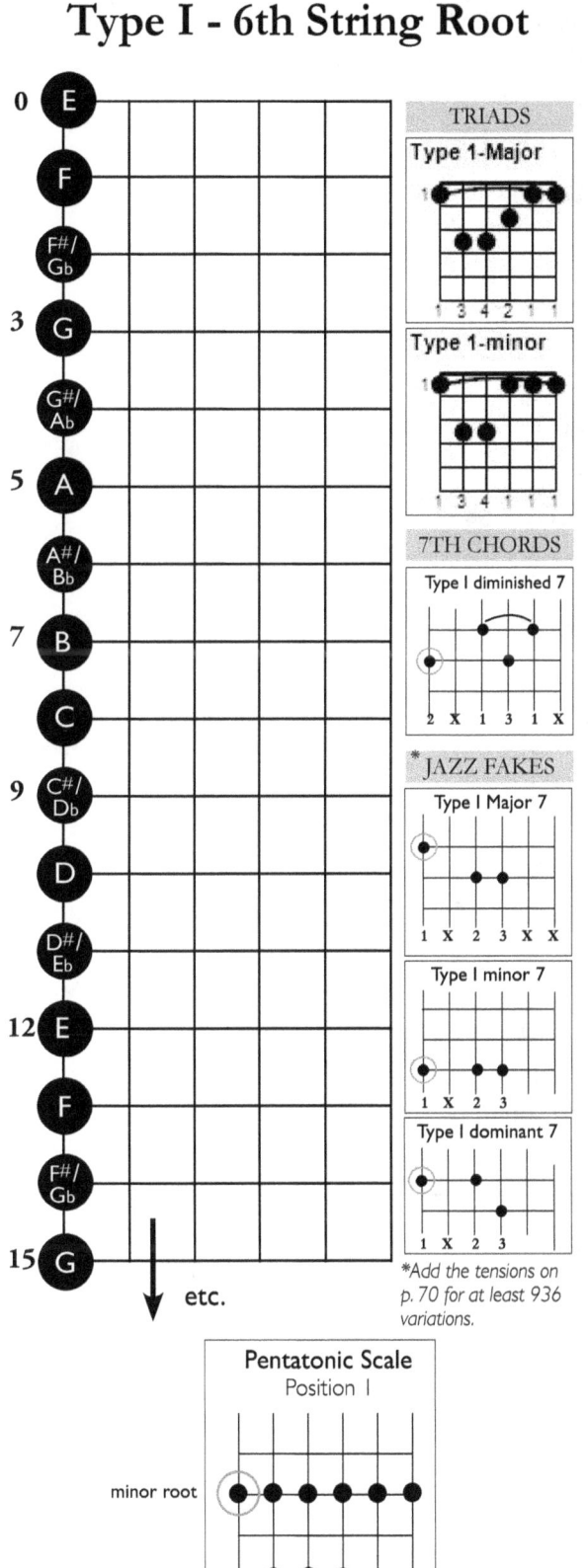

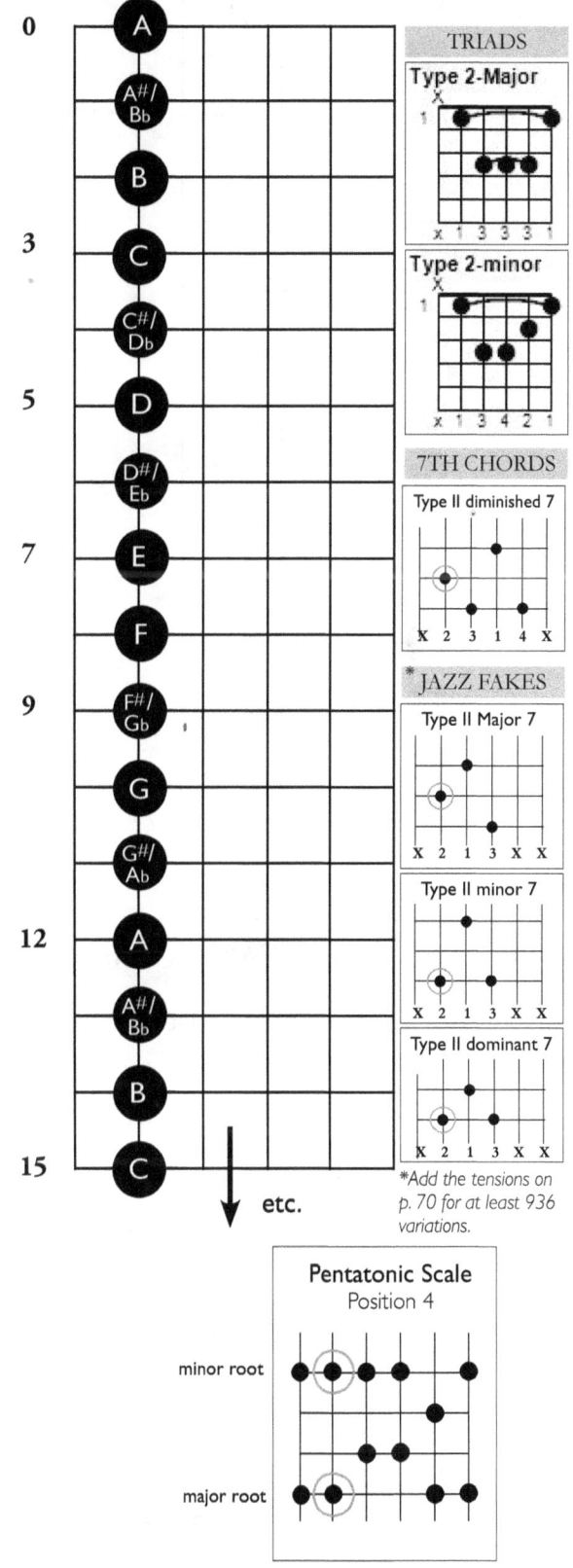

KEY SHAPES WITH SCALE/CHORD DEGREES

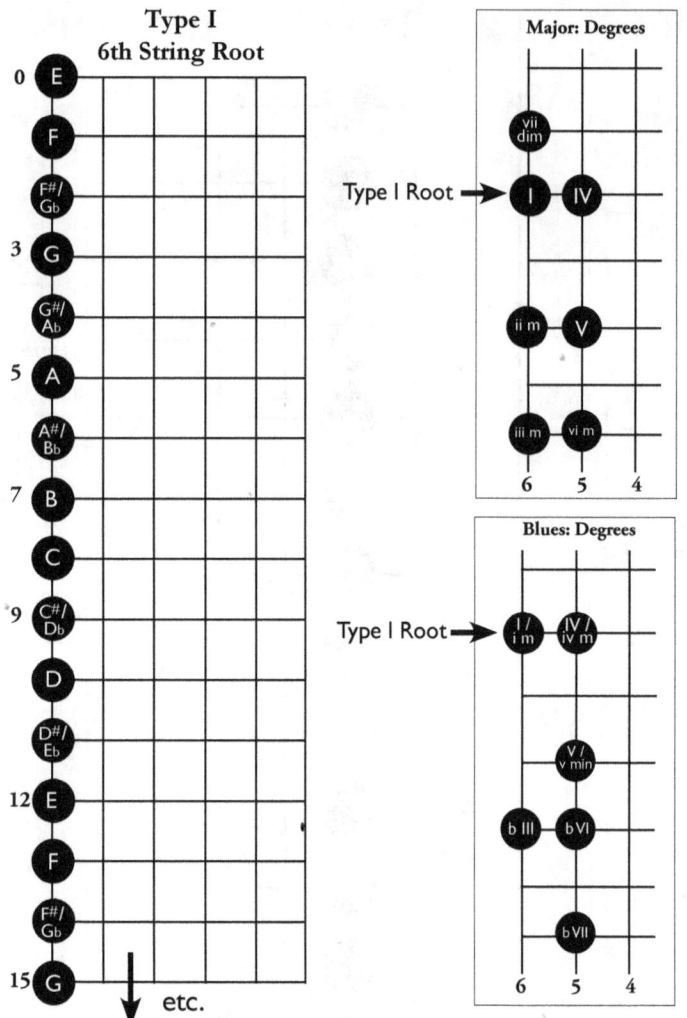

THE FAMOUS FILE CARD!

Optional, in case you actually want to write out everything! Unfortunately, you will have to understand basic theory for this.

SCALE FORMULA	CHORDS	MODES
1	Major	**Major**/Ionian
1	Minor	Dorian
1/2	Minor	Phrygian
1	Major	Lydian
1	Major	Mixolydian
1	Minor	**Minor**/Aeolian
1/2	Diminished	Locrian

Blues Harmony = Parallel Major+Minor Mode

APPENDIX

APPENDIX

TABLATURE

This section has two parts. The first is taken from my first book "No Fail Guitar", and explains basic tablature notation. The second part explains my six performance abbreviations, which are used as needed, above the tab.

BASIC TABLATURE NOTATION

Tablature is an alternative to standard music notation. It works mainly for guitar and bass. Tablature (tab for short), gives an over head view of the fret board. Each of the six lines represents a string, and the numbers written on the line tell what frets to play. You read the numbers from left to right, (not top to bottom). Numbers stacked on top of each other mean you play them together. Tab tells you exactly where to put your fingers on the guitar neck, it doesn't tell you what fingers to use, that's up to you.

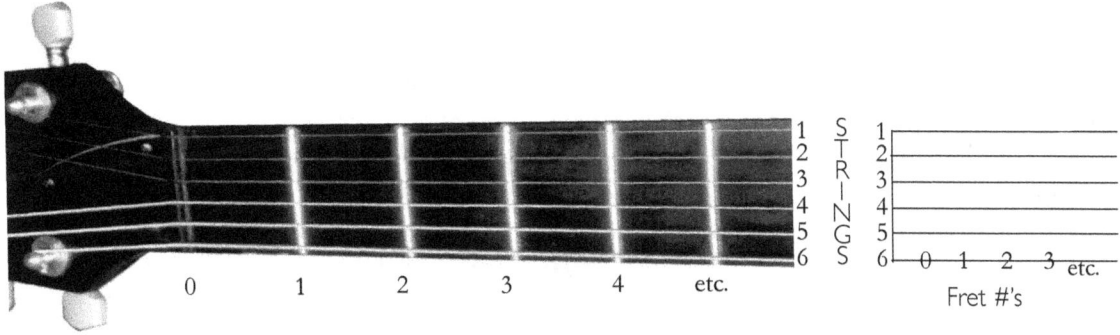

PERFORMANCE ABBREVIATIONS

I use five letters and one sign in my tabs to denote certain performance techniques. Although some are unconventional, both my students and me find them more specific than other ways of notation.

Track #'s 12-19

HAMMER-ON: Pick the first note only, get the second note by hammering down on it *without picking*.

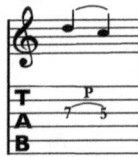

PULL-OFF: Pick the first note only, get the second note by swiping your finger off the first note, in effect picking it.

COMBINED HAMMER & PULL: Examples one and two showed these techniques separately, but they are often combined. Pick only the first note.

BEND: Bend the string to a higher pitch. Unlike other tab, I show the fret that corresponds to the bent note. You don't play the second note/fret, you bend the first note to match. It's a reference.

RELEASE BEND: Relax a *previously bent* note back down to its' starting point. You should already be bent up before you start this one, and release it back down.

COMBINED BEND & RELEASE: Examples four and five showed these techniques separately, but they are often combined. Pick only the first note.

SLIDE: Slide between the two notes indicated.

VIBRATO: The quivering sound on a note. The secret to a good sounding vibrato is *evenness*, push the note up to the same spot, release it and repeat with as even a rhythm as possible. It's fairly easy to do slow, but most people get ragged the faster they go. This is a skill worth mastering, good vibrato is money in the bank.

The curved line between the two notes means you only pick the first note, you get to the second by whatever technique is abbreviated above.

These six techniques are crucial to good sounding, expressive lead. The better you have them down, the better you sound!

UNDERSTAND CHORD DEGREE NAMES

Pros refer to chords by Roman numbers, which tell the chords' place in the key or its degree. The first chord in the key is called the I chord, the fourth chord in the key is called the IV chord, etc. Since a key consists of seven chords, you have seven Roman numbers/degrees. Why do we give chords number names? It makes it easy to change keys! If a song uses a I,IV,V chord progression in the key of C, you can play the I,IV,V chords in the same sequence in the key of G. That's how you change keys! It's just a line by line substitution. Below is a chart of all twelve keys. The Roman numbers are on the top line; upper case Roman numbers mean the chord is major, lower case means minor, lower case plus the degree sign means diminished chord. Below that the chords for all twelve keys are listed.

**Key Names	Professional Chord Names (Gray)/Actual Chords Below						
	I major	ii minor	iii minor	IV major	V major	vi minor	vii°Diminished
A	A	Bmin	C#min	D	E	F#min	G#dim
A#/Bb *	Bb	Cmin	Dmin	Eb	F	Gmin	Adim
B	B	C#min	D#min	E	F#	G#min	A#dim
C	C	Dmin	Emin	F	G	Amin	Bdim
C#/Db *	Db	Ebmin	Fmin	Gb	Ab	Bbmin	Cdim
D	D	Emin	F#min	G	A	Bmin	C#dim
D#/Eb *	Eb	Fmin	Gmin	Ab	Bb	Cmin	Ddim
E	E	F#min	G#min	A	B	C#min	D#dim
F	F	Gmin	Amin	Bb	C	Dmin	Edim
F#/Gb *	Gb	Abmin	Bbmin	Cb	Db	Ebmin	Fdim
G	G	Amin	Bmin	C	D	Emin	F#dim
G#/Ab *	Ab	Bbmin	Cmin	Db	Eb	Fmin	Gdim

*When keys have two possible names (for example, A# or Bb) I have chosen the flat key.
**The chromatic scale and the key names are the same.

Changing keys is easy! Say you're playing a song in the key of G. The chords are; G,D,Em,C. Looking in the chart you notice those chords have the Roman numbers; I,V,vi,IV in the key of G. If you want to change the song to the key of C, just locate the chords that have the same number names in the key of C (I,V,vi,IV chords in C are; C,G,Am,F) and substitute those chords. That's all there is to it!

JAMMING

Jamming successfully has been a challenge for many of my students. After a year or two of playing many are ready to step out and jam with others, only to find out it's harder than it looks. Here is a typical " first jam ":

YOUR FIRST JAM!

Guitarist A meets Guitarist B (at work/school/online,etc). After determining they both like the same kind of music, they agree to get together and jam. When they finally get together for the big jam Guitarist A says, "Do you know how to play song A?" Guitarist B replies " No, do you know how to play song B?" Guitarist A says " No, how about song C?" After another twenty minutes of this pointless back and forth and a half hour of random song bits from both, everybody breaks for a beer and the "jam" is over. It only takes a few jams like this to convince most people to forget jamming and just drink beer instead.

JAM 2.0

You can have a better experience at your jams if you define your goals and prepare. While it's better if both players are at similar levels of competence, you don't have to be identical as long as you can get along. Less proficient players can pick up a lot from better players, who will often put up with them when flattered and plied with free refreshments.

1. **Define your goals:** This will depend on your level of playing ability. Most beginners are not capable of true improvisation, instead jams are like a self help group. Players can help each other learn to play songs together, or learn how to turn a few riffs into a decent solo. Don't be too picky! Even if Jimmy Page is your hero, limiting your scope to Page fanatics only will definitely make jams harder to set up, widen your scope to classic rock fans instead.

2. **Prepare:** If playing songs is your goal, decide on a couple of songs in advance and do your best to learn them first. Bring recorded versions to the jam to serve as a reference and have at it! If learning to solo is the goal, have a few easy songs to jam over. A 12 bar blues, the three chord boogie pattern in the blues chapter, basically any popular, easy to play song with just a few chords. That way you can trade off, with one player trying out his riffs and the other player backing on rhythm. If the jams are simple, even if one player doesn't know the chords they should be able to learn the changes easily.

PLAYING OUT

Easy entry points are private parties, church groups and open mic nights. You want to start with an easy audience, where most people are on your side. Open mic nights at coffee houses can be better than bars, because the audience is mostly sober. I wouldn't start with club gigs, dealing with restless drunks can be a hassle. The best way to start with clubs is to open for another, similar band. You only need ten or twelve songs for an opener.

KEY SECTION

Key of A Major

SCALE	CHORDS	MODES
A	A major	A Ionian/Major
B	B minor	B Dorian
C#	C# minor	C# Phrygian
D	D major	D Lydian
E	E major	E Mixolydian
F#	F# minor	F# Aeolian/Minor
G#	G# diminished	G# Locrian

Blues Key Worksheet
with most commonly used chords from both keys

A BLUES KEY

chords from key of A major	chords from key of A minor/(C major)
A, D, E	C, F, G, A min., D min., E min.

Key of Bb Major

SCALE	CHORDS	MODES
Bb	Bb major	Bb Ionian/Major
C	C minor	C Dorian
D	D minor	D Phrygian
Eb	Eb major	Eb Lydian
F	F major	F Mixolydian
G	G minor	G Aeolian/Minor
A	A diminished	A Locrian

Blues Key Worksheet
with most commonly used chords from both keys

Bb BLUES KEY

chords from key of Bb major	chords from key of Bb minor/(Db major)
Bb, Eb, F	Db, Gb, Ab, Bb min, Eb min, F min

Key of B Major

SCALE	CHORDS	MODES
B	B major	B Ionian/Major
C#	C# minor	C# Dorian
D#	D# minor	D# Phrygian
E	E major	E Lydian
F#	F# major	F# Mixolydian
G#	G# minor	G# Aeolian/Minor
A#	A# diminished	A# Locrian

Blues Key Worksheet
with most commonly used chords from both keys

B BLUES KEY

chords from key of B major	chords from key of B minor/(D major)
B, E, F#	D, G, A, B min, E min, F#min

Key of C Major

SCALE	CHORDS	MODES
C	C major	C Ionian/Major
D	D minor	D Dorian
E	E minor	E Phrygian
F	F major	F Lydian
G	G major	G Mixolydian
A	A minor	A Aeolian/Minor
B	B diminished	B Locrian

Blues Key Worksheet
with most commonly used chords from both keys

C BLUES KEY

chords from key of C major	chords from key of C minor/(Eb major)
C, F, G	Eb, Ab, Bb, C min, F min, G min

Key of Db Major

SCALE	CHORDS	MODES
Db	Db major	Db Ionian/Major
Eb	Eb minor	Eb Dorian
F	F minor	F Phrygian
Gb	Gb major	Gb Lydian
Ab	Ab major	Ab Mixolydian
Bb	Bb minor	Bb Aeolian/Minor
C	C diminished	C Locrian

Blues Key Worksheet
with most commonly used chords from both keys

Db BLUES KEY

chords from key of Db major	chords from key of Db minor/(Fb major)
Db, Gb, Ab	Fb, Bbb, Cb, Db min, Gb min, Ab min

Key of C#* Major

SCALE	CHORDS	MODES
C#	C# major	C# Ionian/Major
D#	D# minor	D# Dorian
E#	E# minor	E# Phrygian
F#	F# major	F# Lydian
G#	G# major	G# Mixolydian
A#	A# minor	A# Aeolian/Minor
B#	B# diminished	B# Locrian

Blues Key Worksheet
with most commonly used chords from both keys

C# BLUES KEY

chords from key of C# major	chords from key of C# minor/(E major)
C#, F#, G#	E, A, B, C# min, F# min, G# min

Key of D Major

SCALE	CHORDS	MODES
D	D major	D Ionian/Major
E	E minor	E Dorian
F#	F# minor	F# Phrygian
G	G major	G Lydian
A	A major	A Mixolydian
B	B minor	B Aeolian/Minor
C#	C# diminished	C# Locrian

Blues Key Worksheet
with most commonly used chords from both keys

D BLUES KEY

chords from key of D major	chords from key of D minor/(F major)
D, G, A	F, Bb, C, D min, G min, A min

* Even though C# and Db are the same keys written enharmonically I have included them to make the blues keys easier to understand. The same goes for F# and Gb.

Key of Eb Major

SCALE	CHORDS	MODES
Eb	Eb major	Eb Ionian/Major
F	F minor	F Dorian
G	G minor	G Phrygian
Ab	Ab major	Ab Lydian
Bb	Bb major	Bb Mixolydian
C	C minor	C Aeolian/Minor
D	D diminished	D Locrian

Blues Key Worksheet
with most commonly used chords from both keys

Eb BLUES KEY

chords from key of Eb major	chords from key of Eb minor/(Gb major)
Eb, Ab, Bb	**Gb, Cb, Db, Eb min, Ab min, Bb min**

Key of E Major

SCALE	CHORDS	MODES
E	E major	E Ionian/Major
F#	F# minor	F# Dorian
G#	G# minor	G# Phrygian
A	A major	A Lydian
B	B major	B Mixolydian
C#	C# minor	C# Aeolian/Minor
D#	D# diminished	D# Locrian

Blues Key Worksheet
with most commonly used chords from both keys

E BLUES KEY

chords from key of E major	chords from key of E minor/(G major)
E, A, B	**G, C, D, E min, A min, B min**

Key of F Major

SCALE	CHORDS	MODES
F	F major	F Ionian/Major
G	G minor	G Dorian
A	A minor	A Phrygian
Bb	Bb major	Bb Lydian
C	C major	C Mixolydian
D	D minor	D Aeolian/Minor
E	E diminished	E Locrian

Blues Key Worksheet
with most commonly used chords from both keys

F BLUES KEY

chords from key of F major	chords from key of F minor/(Ab major)
F, Bb, C	**Ab, Db, Eb, F min, Bb min, C min**

Key of Gb Major

SCALE	CHORDS	MODES
Gb	Gb major	Gb Ionian/Major
Ab	Ab minor	Ab Dorian
Bb	Bb minor	Bb Phrygian
Cb	Cb major	Cb Lydian
Db	Db major	Db Mixolydian
Eb	Eb minor	Eb Aeolian/Minor
F	F diminished	F Locrian

Blues Key Worksheet
with most commonly used chords from both keys

Gb BLUES KEY

chords from key of Gb major	chords from key of Gb minor/(Bbb major)
Gb, Cb, Db	Bbb, Ebb, Fb, Gb min, Cb min, Db min

Key of F#* Major

SCALE	CHORDS	MODES
F#	F# major	F# Ionian/Major
G#	G# minor	G# Dorian
A#	A# minor	A# Phrygian
B	B major	B Lydian
C#	C# major	C# Mixolydian
D#	D# minor	D# Aeolian/Minor
E#	E# diminished	E# Locrian

Blues Key Worksheet
with most commonly used chords from both keys

F# BLUES KEY

chords from key of F# major	chords from key of F# minor/(A major)
F#, B, C#	A, D, E, F# min, B min, C# min

Key of G Major

SCALE	CHORDS	MODES
G	G major	G Ionian/Major
A	A minor	A Dorian
B	B minor	B Phrygian
C	C major	C Lydian
D	D major	D Mixolydian
E	E minor	E Aeolian/Minor
F#	F# diminished	F# Locrian

Blues Key Worksheet
with most commonly used chords from both keys

G BLUES KEY

chords from key of G major	chords from key of G minor/(Bb major)
G, C, D	Bb, Eb, F, G min, C min, D min

Key of Ab Major

SCALE	CHORDS	MODES
Ab	Ab major	Ab Ionian/Major
Bb	Bb minor	Bb Dorian
C	C minor	C Phrygian
Db	Db major	Db Lydian
Eb	Eb major	Eb Mixolydian
F	F minor	F Aeolian/Minor
G	G diminished	G Locrian

Blues Key Worksheet
with most commonly used chords from both keys

Ab BLUES KEY

chords from key of Ab major	chords from key of Ab minor/(Cb major)
Ab, Db, Eb	Cb, Fb, Gb, Ab min, Db min, Eb min

* Even though F# and Gb are the same keys written enharmonically I have included them to make the blues keys easier to understand. The same goes for C# and Db.

VISUAL KEYS/CHORD DEGREES

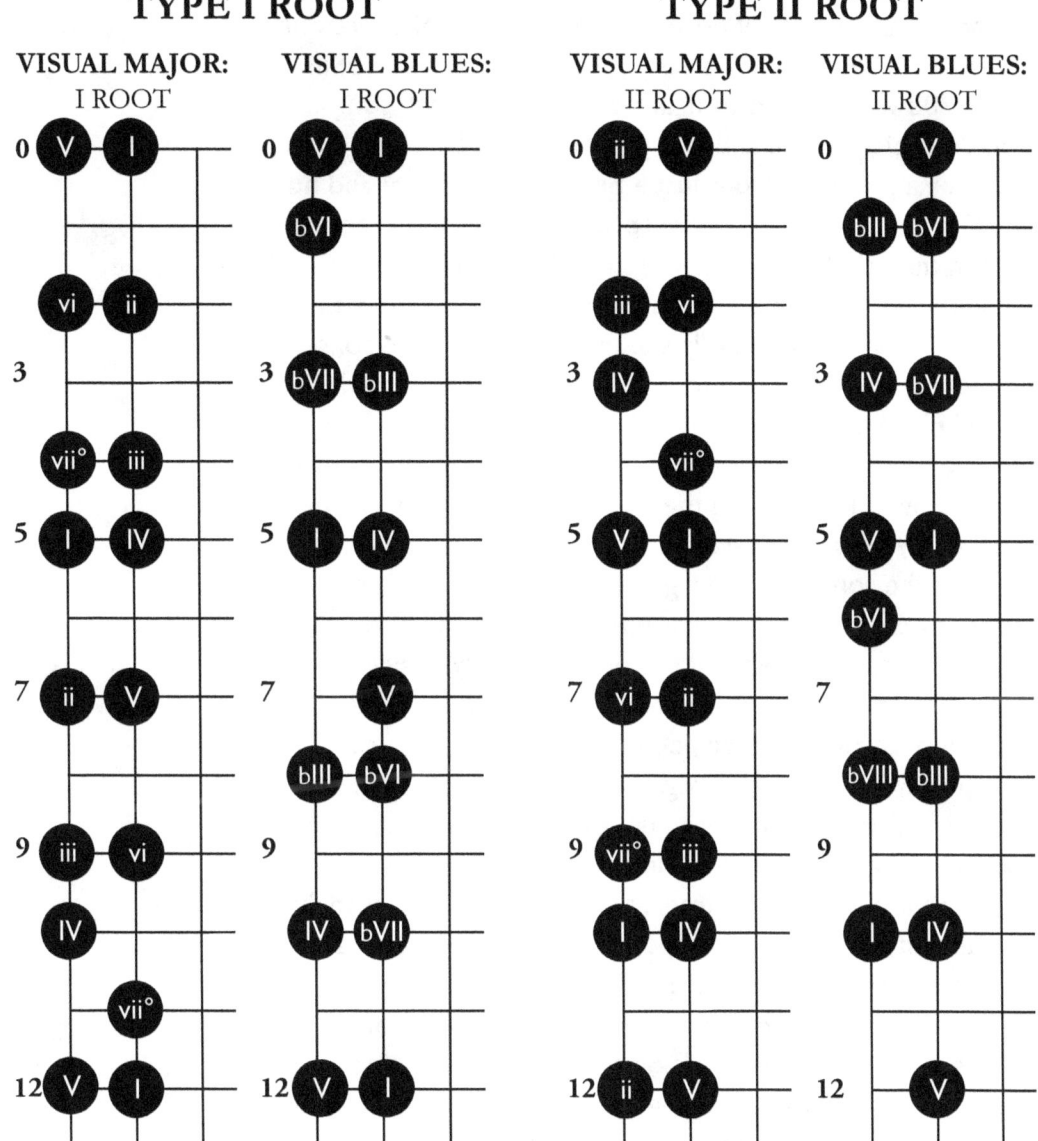

Both Type I and II examples are based on a 5th fret root. This is for illustration only, since the entire pattern can be moved in either direction as explained in the Theory section.

Remember, I, IV, and V chords are both major and minor in blues keys.

SPEED METAL BLUES
(basically any loud, obnoxious rock)

E Blues Scale

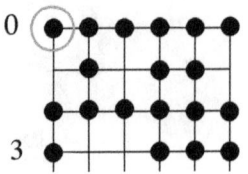

Blues Scale on the 6th String

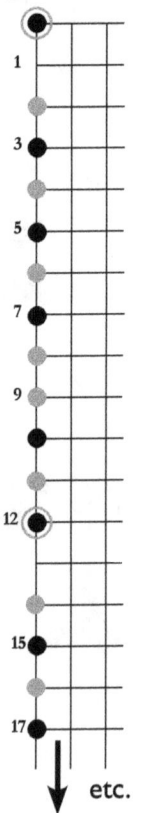

etc.

Many rock songs consist of power chords built off of pentatonic and blues scale roots. This is a style I first became aware of in the early 70's when I tried to figure out Black Sabbath songs. All you do is pick a scale and play power chords built on those notes. Since a power chord is just a perfect 5th interval and not a complete chord, you don't have to worry about those pesky major and minor chords! Also songs in this style are mostly played with lots of volume and distortion, so power chords are plenty huge sounding. Generally the more "normal" the song is, the more it sticks to pentatonic roots. The more "outside" tunes add more extra blues notes. As you might guess with a blues scale having so many options, the only way to keep the key obvious is to keep hitting the root a lot. This explains why so many heavy songs are based in E, you have to keep hitting the root or the song turns into garbage. This means it's easy to tell what key the song is in, (what note do they keep hitting?), but a pain to figure out with all the options. Really heavy bands do this trick with weird scales like diminished, whole tone, synthetic modes, or whatever perverted sequence they can dream up (Slayer). As for soloing, use whatever scale or note sequence the power chords are built on, based on the root they keep hitting. If all else fails, the pentatonic scale is your friend. There are only twelve frets and it has to be one of them! The middle diagram shows an E pentatonic minor/blues scale written on the sixth string. The pentatonic notes are black, and the extra blues tensions are in grey. The bottom example is a simple power chord riff built off the notes in the middle diagram. Notice how I keep hitting the open E root, (try playing the same riff with no root notes to see why.)

Cheesy Metal Riff in E

118 APPENDIX

SUPERIMPOSING MODES
(real world mode use)

Although I explained the basic concept of modal harmony in chapter three of the theory section, it doesn't help much in actual use. This is because most popular songs are in either major (Ionian), minor (Aeolian), or blues keys. Therefore it seems the rest of the modes are useless, unless you come across the rare popular song written in that mode. However it is possible to solo with exotic sounding modes over "normal" songs by superimposing them. (A fancy term for dump on top of.) This because all modes, even the exotic ones, are considered basically major or minor in tonality (except locrian which is diminished). The table below lists the three main harmonic categories; major, minor, and blues followed by the other modes that fit in those categories. I have done this for an E root, since E is a popular key in rock music. Since modes are just major scales, played from a different root, I put the related major keys in parentheses. Also, since blues harmony contains both major and minor tonality, you get twice the fun! This means you can solo in E mixolydian (A major) over a song in E blues, like Purple Haze or Back in Black! A word of caution, once you superimpose modes you are playing a scale that is outside of the original key, whether this sounds cool or ugly is subjective. Until you do this enough to get a sense of what will work and what won't (lydian is not good for country music), I would save this concept for experimentation.

Tonality/Sound	Modes/(Keys)
E Major	E major (E), E lydian (B), E mixolydian (A)
E Minor	E minor (G), E dorian (D), E phrygian (C)*
E Blues	All of the above, but I have the best luck with dorian, mixolydian, and minor modes

*Although phrygian is nominally a minor mode, it sound is so distinctive/weird that you can try it over anything, the same with E locrian (F). Who knows until you try?

FIGURING OUT SONGS

Pick easy songs to start with. By easy I mean simple strumming songs that are mostly guitar mixed up front. Singer-songwriters are good; Bob Dylan, Jimmy Buffet, Taylor Swift. Bands include Creedence, Green Day, early AC/DC, Kiss, even Misfits or Ramones if that's your thing.

Once you have your easy song there are three ways to figure it out; luck, trial and error or experience. Sometimes you can luck into a song, but mostly you have to go with a combination of experience and trial and error. At first it will have to be mostly trial and error! Here is the basic process:

- Start at the first main part of the song, ie. the verse or chorus, skip any intro for now. Once you know the key it will be easier to come back and deal with any intro riffs.

- Focus on the first chord (of verse, etc.) only. Stop the song when the chord changes. The remaining three steps all refer to the first chord only.

- Figure out the bass/root note of the chord. Play notes up and down the sixth string only, from frets zero to twelve. Play only the sixth string, don't skip around! Find the note that best matches the chord. There are twelve notes and it has to be one of them. Play that first chord twelve or more times if you need to, and find the best note to match that chord. Several notes will sound OK, but one will be the best!

- Next, figure out the basic "quality" of the chord (whether it's major, minor or power chord). Try all three kinds and choose the best match.

- Finally choose the best type of chord; type I, type II, or open (if possible). Listen and compare all three types and choose the one that sounds closest.

For example, if the first chord was a D minor. You would first locate the bass/root note on the sixth string, tenth fret. After determining that a minor chord sounded best, you may decide the tenth fret D minor (type I), sounds too dinky and opt to play a type II or open D minor instead.

Congratulations! You just figured out the first chord by 100% trial and error. Now you have to do this process for two or three more chords before you can find this group of chords in a specific key. (You can find one or two chords in several keys, see the theory application chapter.)

Once you know the key, things get a little easier. You still have to use trial and error, but now you have short list of six to nine chords to work from. This means only a few tries to figure out the next chord, not dozens. You also have a scale to work with, to figure out any intro riffs or solos (try position 1 first).

This is why I advise easy songs to start with!

www.ingramcontent.com/pod-product-compliance
Lightning Source LLC
Chambersburg PA
CBHW080517110426
42742CB00017B/3142